My Family Cookbook

My Family Cookbook

Mothers Against Hunger

by

Debbie Stevens

eBooks2go

Your Author Journey Begins Here

Quantity Purchases:
Companies, professional groups, clubs, and other organizations may qualify
for special terms when ordering quantities of this title.
For information, email info@ebooks2go.net,
or call (847) 598-1150 ext. 4141.
www.ebooks2go.net

Published in the United States by eBooks2go, Inc.
1827 Walden Office Square, Suite 260,
Schaumburg, IL 60173

ISBN: 978-1-5457-5473-3

Library of Congress Cataloging in Publication

I am dedicating my family cookbook to Janet Chapman.
Thank you for always telling me I could write this cookbook.
You told me this would be an amazing journey—to always keep writing
and to never give up.

To Melissa Mayhue for always supporting me during this journey and for giving
me advice and sending me a signed copy of your book.
I love your books. You are one my favorite authors.
Thank you both for not letting me give up on writing this cookbook.

To Lynn Kurland for all the wonderful advice you have given me
to make this happen.

To Albertson's for all the inspiration I got while I was shopping
for this cookbook.

To my loving family for always being supportive during this journey
of writing this cookbook.

Conversion Chart

INGREDIENT	1 cup	3/4 cup	2/3 cup	1/2 cup	1/3 cup	1/4 cup	1 Tbsp	1 tsp
Flour	120g	90g	80g	60g	40g	30g	8g	…
Sugar	200g	150g	133g	100g	97g	50g	13g	…
Brown sugar	180g	135g	120g	90g	60g	45g	12g	…
Butter	240g	180g	160g	120g	80g	60g	15g	…
Oats	90g	68g	60g	45g	30g	23g	6g	…
Nuts, chopped	150g	113g	100g	75g	50g	38g	10g	…
Milk/ Cream/ Water	240ml	180ml	160ml	120ml	80ml	60ml	15ml	5ml
Salt, Spices, Herbs, Baking Soda	…	…	…	…	…	…	15ml	5ml

Table of Contents

Breads, Rolls, and Breakfast

Apple Cinnamon Rolls

Ingredients

6 cups of all-purpose flour

2/3 cup of sugar

1 tsp. of salt

4 tbs. of shortening butter flavored

2 packages of yeast

2 1/4 cups of warm water

1 tsp. of cinnamon

4 apples (peeled and diced; add to the apples 1 tsp. of cinnamon, 4 tbs. of sugar, 1 tsp. of vanilla. Mix this up and set it aside until the dough is rolled out)

Directions

Add yeast and hot water together—mixed up and set aside.

In another big bowl, add 3 1/2 cups of flour, sugar, salt, and shortening. Then add yeast mixture and mix up on low so the flour does not go everywhere.

Keep adding the rest of the flour 1 cup at a time until all 6 cups of flour have been added. If you find the dough is a little dry, add a little more water, but no more than 1/4 cup of water.

Place dough in an oiled bowl to rise until it's doubled in size.

Once it has doubled in size, take half the dough and place a floured countertop and roll out to about 2 inches thick, or the thickness your wanting.

Make sure that your rolling pin is also floured as the dough will stick to it.

Christmas butter

Ingredients

1 cup of butter

1 cup of brown sugar

2 tsp. of vanilla

1 tsp. of cinnamon

6 tsp. of margarine (this keeps the Christmas butter soft and useable)

Directions

Mix well until smooth.

After you make the Christmas butter, take a spoon and put on the rolled-out dough. Smooth all over the dough. Be generous as you spread this out because this will melt in the oven on a baking dish as a glaze.

Add the apple mixture to the top of the Christmas butter—be generous with the apples.

Now roll up the dough like you would for cinnamon rolls; pitch it together so it will stay closed.

Cut into 2-inch slices and place on oiled baking dish to rise one more time for about 10 minutes. Once it has risen, place in the oven at 375 degrees for 25 minutes.

When they come out of the oven, flip them over so the melted Christmas butter acts as a glaze on top.

When this is done, it will taste just like hot apple pie. Take the rest of the Christmas butter. If there is any left, melt it and spoon it over the apple cinnamon rolls.

Yields 24 apple cinnamon rolls.

Apple Dumpling Cinnamon Bread

Ingredients

8 Rhodes yeast dinner rolls—cut into 4 pieces

5 apples—peeled, cored, and cut up

1/2 cup of sugar

1/2 brown sugar

1/2 stick of butter

1 tsp. of vanilla

3 tbs. of flour

1 tsp. cinnamon

1/2 canned frosting—melted to drizzle over the top of apple dumpling cinnamon bread when it's done

Directions

Make sure to let yeast dinner rolls defrost, then cut the round yeast balls into four pieces.

Let rise to double their size.

Next, melt butter then add both brown and white sugar, cinnamon, and flour. Set aside.

Peel, core, and cut up the apples, then add in the butter mixture. Mix together.

Now that the yeast pieces have risen and doubled in size, add them to the apple mixture. Stir well.

Take a 9 × 13 pan and spray the pan with nonstick cooking spray.

Pour the apple and yeast mixture into the pan.

Bake at 350 for 35–40 minutes.

Drizzle melted frosting over the top of apple dumpling cinnamon bread.

Let cool.

Serves 12.

Biscuits

Ingredients

2 cups self-rising flour

1 cube of butter

1 tsp sugar

2/3 cup of milk

1 tsp baking powder

Directions

Mix flour, baking powder, sugar and butter together until it is like crumbs. Next stir in the milk until it forms into a dough. Flour the board than knead until it comes together than roll out until desire thickness.

Then use a biscuit cutter to cut out biscuits. bake on sprayed cookie sheet and bake at 350. Bake until golden brown or about 20 minutes.

Serves 8 to 10.

Banana Pancakes

Ingredients

2 cups Bisquick or flour

2 eggs

1 cup of milk

1/4 cup sugar

2 tbs. baking powder

2 tbs. vegetable oil

2 ripe bananas—smashed

1 tsp. cinnamon

1 tsp. of vanilla

1 tsp. allspice

Directions

Mix together eggs, milk, vegetable oil, ripe bananas, cinnamon, vanilla, and allspice mix well.

Add in all the dry ingredients. If it seems to be too thin, then add another 1/2 cup of flour and mix well. The bananas do tend to add liquid to the pancake batter.

Cook the pancakes in 1 tbs. of oil. Wait until bubbles appear on the top of the pancakes, then flip until they are golden on each side. Do this to the rest of the batter until all the pancake batter is used up.

Caramel Apple Cinnamon Biscuit

Ingredients

5 apples—peeled and cored; cut up in small chucks

1/2 cup of sugar

1 tsp. of cinnamon

4 1/2 cups of Bisquick mix—to Bisquick add 1/2 cup of sugar and 1 tsp. of cinnamon

2 cups of water or milk

2 tsp. of vanilla

Directions

Mix up Bisquick mix with 1/2 cup of sugar and 1 tsp. of cinnamon. Stir and add water. The dough will be sticky, so put flour on the counter before you put the dough on top. This way, it doesn't stick. Roll this out as you would for cinnamon rolls. When you get it to the right thickness, put butter all over the top. Sprinkle sugar and cinnamon. Roll it up and cut just as you would a cinnamon roll. Make sure not to roll them out too thick. 1/4 inch should be thick enough.

Apple mixture—cut up 5 apples and peel along with coring them. Put this into a bowl and add 1/2 cup of sugar, 2 tsp. of vanilla, and 1 tsp. of cinnamon. Mix well and set aside. Put into pan. Cook them for about 5 minutes. Drain and set aside.

Spray the bottom of a 13 × 9 pan. Put all the apples all over the bottom of the pan, then place your biscuit cinnamon rolls on top of the apples. Bake at 350 for 30 minutes, or until golden on top. When cooled, find a cookie sheet to fit the 13 × 9 pan. Place on top of it and flip it over. Serve with whipped cream or ice cream.

Serves 10.

Cinnamon Blackberry French Toast

Blackberry Syrup

Ingredients

1 cup of blackberries

1/2 cup blueberries

1 tsp. of vanilla

1 tsp. of cinnamon

1/2 cup of blackberry syrup

1/2 cup sugar

Ingredients

Egg mixture

2 loafs of cinnamon-swirl bread

10 eggs (adjust to the size of your family)

2 cups of milk

2 tsp. of vanilla

1 tsp. of cinnamon

Directions

Cook together until the berries are soft this way it gives the syrup a real blackberry flavor. Cook this for about 7–8 minutes.

Take the french toast and add the Christmas butter (found in this cookbook) on top, then add the blackberry syrup over the top, making sure some of the berries are on top.

Serves 8.

Directions

Mix this up with a mixer until smooth. Take the bread and dip in egg mixture putting it into a frying pan with tbs. of oil. Brown on both sides until golden brown. When you get the french toast all done, put it into the oven to finish the rest of the meal. This will keep it warm.

Cinnamon Rolls

Ingredients

6 cups of all-purpose flour

1/3 cup of sugar

1 tsp. of salt

2 tbs. of shortening butter flavored

2 packages of yeast

2 1/4 cup of warm water

1 tsp. of cinnamon

Directions

Mix yeast and hot water. Set aside.

Now to another big bowl add 3 1/2 cups of flour, sugar, salt, and shortening. Now add yeast mixture and mix up on low so the flour does not go everywhere.

Keep adding the rest of the flour one cup at a time until all 6 cups of flour have been added.

If you find the dough is a little dry add a little more water, but no more than 1/4 cup of water.

Place dough in an oiled bowl to rise until it doubles in size.

Once it has double in size take half the dough and put onto a floured countertop and roll out to about 2 inches thick or the thickness your wanting.

Make sure that your rolling pin is also floured, as the dough will stick to it.

Christmas Butter (for recipe, see page 3).

Christmas Brunch

Directions

How to put it all together: Tear up the bread into pieces and put into a bowl set aside. In another bowl, mix the wet ingredients. Mix the 12 eggs, 1/2 cup french vanilla creamer, 4 cups milk; add cinnamon, vanilla, allspice, and sugar.

Add the torn-up bread to wet ingredients mix with a spoon and make sure that the bread is covered with all the milk mixture. Set in fridge until the next morning. In the morning, cook the sausage and apples together until sausage is done. Drain add in layers. Spray pan 13×9 adding bread mixture first, then add sausage and apple mixture, then another layer of bread mixture until all has be used. Cook at 350 for 45 minutes, or until a knife comes out clean when testing the brunch. Serve with Christmas butter.

Serves 10 people.

Ingredients

2 loafs of cinnamon bread—tore up into small pieces

12 eggs

1 cup sugar

1/2 cup french vanilla creamer—liquid (dried is fine too)

4 cups of milk

3 apples—peeled cored and cut up

2 packs maple-favored sausage—links or ground sausage

1 tsp. baking powder

2 tsp. vanilla

1 tsp. allspice

2 tsp. cinnamon

Christmas Butter–Spiced Muffins

Directions

Cream together sugar, eggs, shortening, then add creamer, vanilla, nutmeg, cinnamon, allspice, ginger and mix together.

Then add in your dry ingredients and mix in the flour slowly so it doesn't go everywhere.

You can either make this as a cake or muffins.

Get you muffin tins out and spray them with nonstick cooking spray, then add cake mix to each tin, filling it over halfway.

Bake at 350 for 10–15 minutes.

Christmas Butter (for recipe, see page 3).

Ingredients

1 1/2 cup of sugar

2 eggs

1/2 cup of butter-flavored shortening

1 cup of Cinnabon coffee creamer (liquid)

1 tsp. of vanilla

1 tsp. of nutmeg

2 tsp. of cinnamon

1 tsp. allspice

1 tsp. ginger

2 tsp. of baking powder

**2 cups of flour or cake flour
(note: sift the flour)**

French Toast

Caramel Apples

Ingredients

6 apples—peeled and cored (slice thin)

1 cup of brown sugar

1/4 cup of maple syrup

1 tsp. of vanilla

4 tsp. of butter

Directions

Mix all this together and put it into a pan cook until apples and sauce thicken. When the sauce is all done pour over the french toast. Top with whipped cream and enjoy the treat as this melt in your mouth.

Serves 10.

Ingredients

6 eggs

2 tsp. of cinnamon

1 tsp. of vanilla

3 cups of milk

1/2 cup of french vanilla creamer—liquid or powdered

1 tsp. of allspice

Directions

Cinnamon swirl bread two loafs (adjust the loafs of bread to family size).

Mix all ingredients together. Now you can use bread or croissants to make the french toast. Dip bread into egg mixture, then cook until golden brown. Can be served with syrup and butter, or it can be served with Christmas butter.

Garlic, Butter, and Herb Rolls

Ingredients

Bread

6 cups of all-purpose flour all

2/3 cup of sugar

1 tsp. of salt

4 tbs. of butter-flavored shortening butter flavored

2 packages of yeast

2 1/4 cups of warm water

Garlic, Butter, and Herb Mixture

3 cloves of garlic—cut up fine or minced

1 tsp. of rosemary—cut up fine

1 tsp. of thyme—cut up fine

2 tbs. of butter—melted with garlic and herbs

Directions for Bread

Add yeast and hot water together mixed up and set aside.

In another big bowl, add 3 1/2 cups of flour, sugar, salt, shortening, now add yeast mixture and stir up.

Keep adding the rest of the flour one cup at a time until all 6 cups of flour have been added.

Knead a couple of times to form the dough on a floured board. Don't knead more than a couple of times, as it will make the dough tough.

Place dough in an oiled bowl to rise, or until it doubles in size.

Once it has doubled in size, take half the dough and put onto a floured countertop and roll out to about 2 inches thick or the thickness your wanting.

Make sure that your rolling pin is also floured, as the dough will stick to it.

Garlic, Butter, and Herb Mixture

Cut up garlic fine, as you don't want big chunks of garlic in the rolls. Next cut up the herbs.

Then add in the butter put in the microwave for less than 30 seconds. Set it aside.

Smooth garlic mixture all over the dough be generous as you spread this out. Now rolled up the dough like you would for cinnamon rolls. Pitch it together so it will stay closed.

Cut into 2-inch slices and place on oiled baking dish to rise one more time about 10 minutes.

Brush with leftover garlic mixture over the top of rolls.

Once it has risen, place in the oven at 350 for 25 minutes.

Monkey Bread

Ingredients

6 cups of all-purpose flour

2/3 cup of sugar

1 tsp. of salt

2 tbs. butter

2 packages of yeast

2 1/4 of warm water

1 tsp. of cinnamon

Directions for Bread

Add yeast and hot water together mixed up and set aside.

Now to another big bowl add 3 1/2 cups of flour, sugar, salt, butter, and cinnamon. Add yeast mixture and mix up on low so the flour does not go everywhere.

Keep adding the rest of the flour one cup at a time until all 6 cups of flour have been added. If you find the dough is a little dry, add a little more water, but no more than 1/4 cup of water.

Place dough in an oiled bowl to rise until it doubled in size.

Get 2 tbs. of butter and melt it set it aside.

Now take 1/2 sugar and 3 tbs. cinnamon stir together.

Now take the bread and start pulling enough dough off to make a small ball.

Dip into butter and in sugar and cinnamon.

I coated the bread pan with melted butter; then a layer of cinnamon balls, chopped nuts, and chocolate chips; and then second layer of nuts and chocolate chips.

Put into the oven for 35 minutes, then add butter on top to soften the monkey bread.

Sausage and Apple Pancakes

Directions

Cook all the sausage and apples together until sausage is done. Now add in your brown sugar and cook for a few more minutes. Drain and set aside.

Mix all the sausage mixture into the pancake batter.

Cook the pancakes in a tbs. of oil and brown on each side.

When done, put into the oven for about 10 minutes on about 200. This will make sure the pancakes are done. Serve with maple syrup. I serve this with Christmas butter.

Serves 8.

Ingredients

For Pancakes

4 cups pancake mix

2 2/3 cup water

2 eggs

1 tsp. baking powder

1/4 cup oil

1 tsp. vanilla

Mix pancake mixture together and set aside

Sausage Mixture

2 maple-flavored sausage—16 oz.

2 peeled and cored apples – diced up

1 tbs. of brown sugar

Sausage and Egg Sandwich

Ingredients

2 packages ground maple-flavored sausage (use the sausage you love)

1 egg—per sandwich

1 slice of cheese—per sandwich

1 tsp. of basil—for garnish is optional

2 slices of bread per sandwich—toasted

1 tsp. mayo—on the bread

Directions

Form sausage into patties and cook on both sides until done. Add cheese so it gets melted. Set them aside.

Over easy egg is what I used. Fry as many as you're going to need for serve everyone.

Toast the bread in the toaster for as many sandwiches as you're going to make.

Take toasted bread and add mayo (or condiments you love).

Add two sausage patties.

Next, add the over easy egg.

Then garnish with basil.

Put this all together and put the top piece of bread on top.

Serves 6.

Sausage Roll Up

Ingredients

4 stocks of celery—cut up finely

1 onion—chopped

3 maple-favored sausage—ground (16 oz.)

1 tsp. basil—cut up

1 tsp. oregano—cut up

carrots—shredded (2 cups)

frozen bread dough or homemade—3 frozen bread doughs thawed and let rise

Directions

Add a little olive oil to moisten the bottom of the pan, but just a little because the sausage already has fat in it. Cook celery, onion, 3 rolls of maple-favored sausage, basil, oregano, and carrots together in a frying pan. Drain fat out of frying pan when the sausage is done. Set aside.

Take the risen bread dough put it on a floured board and roll out to desired thickness. After you have it the way you want it, take meat mixture and put it in the middle of the rolled-out bread dough. Make sure you put a generous amount of meat mixture in the middle of the dough.

Roll it up as you would a cinnamon roll. Pinch the opening together so it seals. Turn over to pinched side. Here comes the fun part: Slice as you would a cinnamon roll—about 2 inches. Hold the bottom so the filling doesn't fall out. Put on a sprayed cookie sheet cook at 350 degrees for 20–25 minutes, or until bread is golden brown. Take melted butter and pour over the top.

Serves 15.

Yeast Rolls

Ingredients

6 cups of all-purpose flour all

2/3 cup of sugar

1 tsp. of salt

2 tbs. butter

2 packages of yeast

2 1/4 of warm water

Directions for Bread

Add yeast and hot water together. Stir up and set aside.

In another big bowl, add 3 1/2 cups of flour, sugar, salt, and butter. Now add yeast mixture and stir together slowly. That way, flour does not go everywhere.

Keep adding the rest of the flour 1 cup at a time until all 6 cups of flour have been added. If you find the dough is a little dry, add a little more water, but no more than 1/4 cup of water. Kneed the bread on floured board for a couple of minutes, or until dough is smooth and combined.

Place dough in an oiled bowl to rise until it doubles in size.

Bread—If you are making bread, then put into greased loaf pan to rise one more time. Then into the oven at 350 for 25–35 minutes until golden brown.

Rolls—Once the dough has doubled in size, now roll out on floured board. Then fold in half and then roll out again.

When you roll this dough out, make sure it's about 1–2 inches thick.

Take a cookie cutter or a glass. Put the edge of the glass in flour, then cut out the rolls.

Place them in a baking dish that has been sprayed which is 13 x 9. This should make 24 rolls. Use two baking dishes for the rolls.

Once you place the rolls in the baking dishes, cover them back up and let rise one more time.

Brush with a little butter before baking.

Once they have risen again, bake at 350 for 20 minutes, or until brown.

White Bread

Ingredients

6 cups of all-purpose flour—keep one cup to roll it out and kneed

2/3 cup of sugar

1 tsp. of salt

3 tbs. butter

2 packages of yeast

2 1/4 cups of warm water

Directions for Bread

Add yeast and warm water together. Stir up and set aside.

In another big bowl, add 3 1/2 cups of flour, sugar, salt, and butter. Add yeast mixture and stir together slowly. That way, flour does not go everywhere.

Keep adding the rest of the flour one cup at a time, until all 5 cups of flour have been added. If you find the dough is a little dry, add a little more water, but no more than a 1/4 cup of water.

With the last cup of flour add some to the board your putting your bread on to, to knead the bread for about 5 minutes.

Place dough in an oiled bowl to rise until it doubled in size.

Place into the oven at 350 for 25–35 minutes, or until golden brown. Butter the top of bread on the outside so the crust is soft. Set on wire rack to cool.

Desserts
Cakes, Pies, and Cookies

Blackberry Cobbler

Ingredients

For Berries

6 cups of blackberries—washed and dried

1 cup sugar

2 tbs. of blackberry syrup

1/2 cup flour

For Cake

2 eggs

1 tsp. of vanilla

1 tsp. of cinnamon

1 1/2 cup of sugar

1/2 cup of butter—room temperature

1 cup of milk

1 tsp. of vanilla

1 tsp. of cinnamon

2 tsp. of baking powder

2 cups of flour or cake flour

Directions for Blackberries

Stir the blackberries, sugar, vanilla, and cinnamon, and the blackberry syrup, flour, and stir together and set aside.

Directions for the Cake

Mix cream with sugar, eggs, vanilla, cinnamon, and baking powder. Add the flour slowly. After it's all mixed together, grease a 13×9 baking dish. Add cake to the pan and add the blackberries on top of the cake.

Mix together 2 tbs. of sugar and 1 tsp. of cinnamon. Stir together for the topping, then sprinkle mixture over the top of the blackberry cobbler. After it is cooled, serve with whipped cream or ice cream. My family loves this when I make this.

Bake at 350 for 35–45 minutes.

Servers 8.

Blackberry Crisp

Topping

Ingredients

2 cups of flour—mix in slowly as not to get flour cloud

1 cup of oats

2 cups of brown sugar

1 tsp. of cinnamon

2 tsp. of vanilla

2 cups of butter—cut in the cold butter

Directions

Mix all together until its crumbly and easy to use. Make up the blackberry mixture and put into a sprayed 13 × 9 baking pan.

Add the topping over the top of the berry mixture, making sure you're covering the berries. Make sure all the edges are covered, as the topping tends to shrink when baking.

Here's how to make the topping crunchy

Ingredients

2 tbs. of sugar

1 tsp. of cinnamon

Directions

Mix this together, then add over the top of the topping and be generous all over the blackberry crisp.

Bake this at 350 for 25 minutes.

Serves 10.

Ingredients

berry mixture

10 cups of blackberries—washed and patted dried

1 1/2 cups of sugar—if the berries are tart to the taste, add 2 cups of sugar

1/2 cup of flour

1 tsp. of vanilla

1 tsp. of cinnamon

1 tsp. of corn starch

Directions

Make the berry mixture up just before you're ready to put it in the baking dish. This way, the berries have time to soak up the flour and the corn starch.

Chocolate Chip Cookies

Directions

Mix together cream, butter, sugars, vanilla, cinnamon, eggs, baking powder, baking soda. Now add in all dry ingredients slowly as not to cause a big mess. Add chocolate chips and mix well. Cool in the fridge for about 30 minutes to let dough set.

Spray a cookie sheet with cooking spray.

Take 1 tsp. full of dough and roll it up and put it on the cookie sheet, using up all the dough. Bake 350 for 9–10 minutes.

Yields 24.

Ingredients

3/4 cup of sugar

3/4 cup of brown sugar

2 eggs

1 tsp. vanilla

1 cup of butter or butter flavored shortening

1/2 cup peanut butter

1 bag chocolate chips

2 1/4 cup flour

1 tsp. baking powder

1 tsp. of baking soda

2 tsp. cinnamon

Chocolate Chip Cookie Ice Cream Sandwiches

Ingredients

3/4 cup of sugar

3/4 cup of brown sugar

2 eggs

1 tsp. vanilla

3/4 cup peanut butter

1 bag chocolate chips

2 1/4 cups flour

1 cup butter or Crisco butter-flavored shortening

1 tsp. baking powder

1 tsp. of baking soda

2 tsp. cinnamon

1 carton of french vanilla ice cream

24 square pieces of foil

Directions

Add cream together with butter, sugar, vanilla, cinnamon, eggs, baking powder, and baking soda. Add in all dry ingredients slowly. Add chocolate chips and mix well. Cool in the fridge for about 30 minutes to let dough set.

Spray a cookie sheet with cooking spray.

Take a tablespoon full of dough and roll it up and put it on the cookie sheet. You want your cookies large enough to hold a scoop of ice cream.

Bake at 350 for 9–10 minutes.

After cookies have cooled, take a cookie and add a scoop of ice cream to the top, then add another cookie on top. Wrap the ice cream sandwich in foil and place it in the freezer in a freezer bag. Do this for all 24 cookies.

Christmas Butter (for recipe, see page 3).

Fruit Bread Pudding

Ingredients

10 croissants—torn into small pieces

3 1/2 cups of milk

3 eggs—lightly beaten

2 cups of sugar

1 1/2 tbs. of vanilla

1 tsp. cinnamon

1/2 tsp. ground nutmeg

2 cups of peaches—peeled and sliced (any fruit you want)

1 tsp. of baking powder

Directions

Place croissants in a bowl. Add milk and let soak for 10 minutes. Mix together eggs, sugar, cinnamon, nutmeg, and baking powder. Pour this over the bread and mix well with your hands.

Now add the peaches and mix it in with your hands. Place in a slightly greased 13 × 9–inch pan. Spread evenly.

Bake at 350 for 50–55 minutes, or until golden brown.

Note: you can use any kind of fruit with this bread pudding.

Serves 15.

Mexican Wedding Cookies

Ingredients

1 cup soften butter

1 tsp. baking powder

3/4 cup powdered sugar—another cup of powdered sugar for rolling the cookies in after baking

2 tsp. vanilla

2 cups flour

1 cup chopped walnuts

Directions

Cream together butter, vanilla, and sugar. In the dry ingredients, add sifted flour and baking powder. Add to butter mixture and walnuts and mix up. Chill for about 20 minutes, then place on greased cookie sheet at 350 degrees for about 9≠10 ten minutes.

When they are done, place on wire rack and let cool for a minute, then roll twice into powdered sugar to cover the cookie.

Yields 24 cookies.

Orange Coffee Cake

Ingredients

1 1/2 cup of sugar

2 eggs

1/2 cup of shortening butter flavored

1 cup of milk

1 tsp. of vanilla

1 tsp. of nutmeg

1 tsp. of cinnamon

1 tsp. allspice

2 tsp. of baking powder

2 cups of flour or cake flour (sift the flour)

2 tbs. of orange zest

Directions

Cream together shortening and sugar, then add eggs, milk, vanilla. Slowly add flour so you don't create a big flour cloud. Add in all the spices. Mix together until creamy.

Christmas Butter (for recipe, see page 3).

Orange and Blueberry Muffins

Ingredients

1 1/2 cup of sugar

2 eggs

1/2 cup of butter-flavored shortening

1 cup of milk

1 tsp. of vanilla

1 tsp. of nutmeg

1 tsp. of cinnamon

1 tsp. allspice

2 tsp. of baking powder

2 cups of flour or cake flour (note: sift the flour)

1/2 cup of blueberries

2 tbs. of orange zest

Directions

Cream together shortening and sugar, then add eggs, milk, and vanilla. Slowly add flour and dry ingredients. Add in all the spices. Fold in blueberries with a big spoon.

Christmas Butter (for recipe, see page 3).

Peach Upside-Down Cobbler

Ingredients

5 peaches—sliced

1/2 cup of brown sugar

1 1/2 cup of sugar

2 eggs

1/2 cup of butter-flavored shortening

1 cup of milk

2 tsp. of vanilla

1 tsp. of nutmeg

1 tsp. of cinnamon

1/2 tsp. ginger

2 tsp. of baking powder

2 cups of flour or cake flour
(note: sift the flour)

Directions

Cream 1 1/2 cup of sugar, 2 eggs, 1/2 cup of butter-flavored shortening, 1 cup of milk, 1 tsp. of vanilla, 1 tsp. of nutmeg, 1 tsp. of cinnamon, 1/2 tsp. ginger. Mix all of this together. Add all the dry ingredients to this mix slowly.

Take the peaches and peel and cut them up add. Add your brown sugar, vanilla, tsp. of cinnamon, nutmeg, and mix all of this together.

Take a baking dish smaller than a 13 × 9 spray the bottom of the pan put all the peach mixture at the bottom of the pan. Then take the cobbler and put over the top of the peaches. Bake for 35–45 minutes at 350 degrees.

When it comes out of the oven, you must take it out of the baking dish by placing a cookie sheet over the top of the cobbler. Flip it over. The cobbler will come right out of the pan without any problems. Serve with ice cream or whipped cream.

Serves 8.

Peanut Butter Cookies

Directions

Cream together butter, sugars, vanilla, cinnamon, eggs, peanut butter, peanut butter flavoring. Mix in baking soda and baking powder to dry ingredients. Mix all together until cookie batter is smooth.

Cool in the fridge for about 30 minutes to let dough set.

Spray a cookie sheet with cooking spray.

Take a tablespoon full of dough and roll it up. Put a fork on it and put it on a cookie sheet.

Bake 350 for 9–10 minutes.

Yields 24 cookies.

Ingredients

3/4 cup of sugar

3/4 cup of brown sugar

2 eggs

1 tsp. peanut butter flavoring

1 cup peanut butter

2 1/4 cup flour

1 cup butter or Crisco butter flavor shortening

1 tsp. baking powder

1 tsp. of baking soda

2 tsp. cinnamon

Strawberry Shortcake

Now for the cake

Ingredients

1 1/2 cup of sugar

1/2 cup of butter-flavored shortening

1 cup of milk

1 tsp. of raspberry flavoring

2 tsp. of baking powder

2 cups of flour—sifted

1 small box of strawberry Jell-O

2 eggs

Directions

Cream together shortening, butter, and sugar, then add eggs, milk, and raspberry flavoring. Add in the box of strawberry Jell-O and mix well, then slowly add flour. The batter will taste like strawberries.

Spray the bottom of a 13 × 9 pan with cooking spray so this doesn't stick to the bottom of the pan.

350 for about 40–45 minutes.

Take the cake out of the pan and place on a cake cooling rack to cool. After it is cooled, cut into slices and place in small bowls. Take the strawberries and spoon a big spoonful over the cake in the bowl. Add whipped cream.

Serves 10.

Ingredients

4 pints of strawberries—sliced up

1 tsp. raspberry flavoring

1/2 cup of sugar

2 cans of ready whipped cream or Cool Whip

1 small box of strawberry Jell-O

Directions for Strawberries

Take the strawberries and stir in the raspberry flavoring and cup of sugar. Set in the fridge until the shortcake is ready to serve.

Main Dishes

Beef, Chicken, Seafood—Fish & Shrimp, Pork

Beef

BBQ Hamburgers

BBQ Sauce

Ingredients

1/2 cup honey BBQ sauce

1/2 cup of brown sugar

2 tbs. of molasses

2 tbs. of hoisin sauce

1 tsp. soy sauce

1/2 tsp. of sesame seed oil (a very little goes a long way)

Directions

Cook the BBQ sauce for a couple of minutes to marry all the favors together. Pour the BBQ sauce over the patties and put into the oven for about 10 minutes so the BBQ sauce can get into all the parts of the patties.

Bake at 350 for 10 minutes.

Serves 10.

Ingredients

2 pounds of hamburger

2 tsp. of basil—cut up fresh works the best

1 tsp. of thyme—I used dried

1 egg

1 tsp. of Italian seasoning

1 cup of breadcrumbs or panko bread—crumbs both works well for this

1 onion—chopped

1 tsp. of oregano—cut up

Directions

Mix all the ingredients together and form into patties and fry them until done. Set them aside until the BBQ sauce is done.

Beef Roast

Ingredients

1 beef roast (you choose the size)

french onion soup

4 onions—cut up

1 tsp. of thyme

1 clove of garlic—cut up

1 tsp. basil—cut up

1 tbs. of olive oil

1 32-oz. beef stock

Directions

Prepare the french onion soup, which will take about 2 hours. Brown the onions in the olive oil with the herbs when they get soft take out of pan. Set aside. Brown the roast in all the herbs that was left in the frying pan while cooking the onions, thyme, garlic, basil. Brown on both sides so you get a nice brown on the outside. Take roast out of the frying pan and put into roasting pan. Add beef stock to onions and herbs cook for about 10 minutes.

Put the roast in a roasting pan and pour the french onion soup over the top. Bake at 350. Bake for 5 hours. Cover with tinfoil. This will fall apart.

Serves 10, depending on the roast you buy.

Beef Soft Taco

Directions

Take the meat and add the basil, oregano, thyme, garlic powder, rosemary, 1 chopped onion, and olive oil. Cook in frying pan. Cook on medium heat until meat is done. Now add the half spaghetti sauce package to the meat and stir in and set aside.

Take a soft taco shell or tortilla shell and start filling this taco with all kinds of goodies. There's chopped avocados, chopped tomatoes, and chopped onions. Sprinkle on some grated cheese. Top with honey and ranch.

Ingredients

2 lbs. hamburger

4 avocados—chopped

4 tomatoes—chopped

1 package of soft taco shells

2 onions—chopped

1 cup of grated cheese—sprinkle over the top

2 cups of lettuce—chopped

2 tsp. oregano—fresh

2 tsp. of fresh basil—chopped

2 tsp. of fresh rosemary—chopped

1 tsp. of garlic powder

Salt to taste

2 tsp. of olive oil

1 tsp. of thyme

1/2 package spaghetti sauce

Beef Stew

Ingredients

6 cut-up chuck steaks

6 carrots—sliced

1 tsp. rosemary—cut up

5 potatoes—peeled and cut up

1 tsp. of basil

2 garlic cloves—peeled and cut up

4 stalks of celery—cut up

2 32-oz. containers of beef stock

1 12-oz. bag of mixed vegetables—broccoli, carrots, cauliflower

2 tbs. beef paste

Salt and pepper to taste

Directions

Cut up the steaks or stew meat, then flour all the meat. The flour will thicken the stew as it cooks. Brown in 2 tbs. of oil, making sure to brown on both sides. Drain off the oil and add meat back into same pan.

Now pour in the beef stock, beef paste. Add in fresh rosemary cut up, dice onions, cut up basil add all in the pan. Cut up the celery, add in a couple of sliced up carrots. This will add favor. Cook this for about 1 hour on medium heat. Now add in potatoes cook until almost done, then add in broccoli, carrots, and cauliflower. Cook until veggies are done. Which is another 20 minutes. Serve with hot biscuits.

Serves 8–10.

Bruschetta

Directions

Take the Texas toast and put it in the oven for 5–6 minutes, or until golden brown. Next cut up the basil set aside. Chop up the tomato and slice the avocado set it aside.

Take the mushrooms and put into a frying pan. Lightly brown them along with the basil. Only for a few minutes. When they are done, put on paper towel to drain.

For the bruschetta, put on the mushrooms first, then add tomato. Avocado is next sliced up. I added a bit more tomato on top, and here's the best part: sprinkle hoisin sauce over the top.

Ingredients

2 slices of garlic-flavored Texas toast

10 sliced up mushrooms

1 tomato—chopped

1 sliced up avocado

1 tsp. of basil—fresh is always better and gives this dish so much flavor

hoisin sauce—just sprinkle lightly

Burritos

In another frying pan, fry the shells a little on each side to get the oil on both sides. No more than a minute. Preheat the oven to 350. Take a cookie sheet and spray with a cooking spray. Take the plate that has the shells on it add bean mixture, then add grated cheese on top. Roll up shells. Put them on cookie sheet and place in the oven. This is a dish you must babysitter, otherwise it could burn.

When they are golden brown, take them out of the oven.

Serves 8–10.

Ingredients

1 pound of hamburger

1 onion—chopped

1 tsp. of basil

1 family-sized can refried beans—40 oz

1 large bag of medium cheddar cheese (you can use any cheese you wish for your tastes.)

1 bag of floured tortillas—24 in bag

sliced black olives—6 oz

Directions

Break up the hamburger. Put in frying pan with basil, onion, and brown until the hamburger is done. Drain hamburger and add to large pot with refried beans. You might want to add 1/4 can of water to the beans as it helps the beans easier to work with.

Salsa

Ingredients

4 tomatoes—chopped

1 onion—chopped

2 stalks of celery—chopped

1 tsp. basil—fresh, chopped

2 tbs. cilantro—chopped

2 avocados—cut up

Directions

Mix together and serve over the top of the burritos with sour cream.

Chili Burgers (Spicy)

Ingredients

2 lbs. of ground hamburger

2 onions—chopped

1 tsp. oregano

1 tsp. of basil

1 tsp. of garlic

2 cups canned stewed tomatoes

2 cans of red kidney beans—drained

1 tbs. of cumin

1 tbs. of chili powder

1 16-oz. tomato sauce

2 cups grated up cheese—set in a bowl to sprinkle on top of each chiliburger

1/2 small can of green peppers—optional

Buns—hamburger buns

Directions

Burgers

2 lbs. of hamburgers, 1 chopped onion, 1 tsp. oregano, 1 tsp. of basil, 1 tsp. of garlic, 1 tsp. of Italian seasoning make this mixture into burgers and fry them up until done set on baking pan in oven on warm to keep them warm. Until chili is done.

Chili

1 tsp. of basil, 1 tsp. of garlic, 2 cups canned stewed tomatoes, 2 cans of red kidney beans, cumin, chili powder, 1 16 oz. tomato sauce, 1 chopped onion, 1/2 can of green peppers. Mix all of this up together and let cook for about 4 hours to get all the herbs marry together. If it needs more chili powder, then add another tsp.

Get the hamburger buns out and add the cooked hamburgers to the bun, then add the chili over the top of the burger. Then add chopped onions and sprinkle with cheese. Put on the top bun.

Serves 10.

Corned Beef Stew

Directions

In a big roasting pan, put the cut-up corn beef, 6 cut-up carrots, 6 cut-up potatoes, 1 cut-up onion, 6 cut-up celery stalks, 1 tsp. of caraway seeds, 1 tsp. of Italian seasoning, 1 tsp. of garlic powder, 1 tsp. of basil, one package of brown gravy, 1/2 of cabbage shredded up, 1/2 of purple cabbage shredded up. Put into the oven and bake at 350 for 1 hour, or until the potatoes and carrots are done or tender.

Serves 8.

Ingredients

Cut up corned beef into chucks (leftover from the Irish corned beef)

2 32-oz. cans of beef stock

6 carrots—cut up

6 potatoes—cut up

1 onion—cut up

6 celery stalks—cut up

1 tsp. of caraway seeds

1 tsp. of Italian seasoning

1 tsp. of garlic powder

1 tsp. of basil

1 package of brown gravy

1/2 of cabbage

1/2 of purple cabbage

Foil Packs of Steaks

Directions

Marinade for Steaks

Cut up the steaks into chunks, with a little of olive oil, 2 tsp. of basil, 1 chopped onion, 1 tsp. oregano, Italian seasoning, 1/2 cup hoisin sauce. Add polish sausage and mushrooms to this mix. Stir this all up and set into the fridge until you're ready to use them.

Take and boil up corn, potatoes, broccoli, carrots all in one pot for about 7 minutes so they aren't all the way cooked and drain them. Add them to the meat mixture to put into the foil packs. Add more of the hoisin sauce to each foil pack. Just sprinkle about a tsp. of hoisin sauce over the top. Close up the foil packs. Bake on a cookie sheet at 350 for 35 minutes.

Serves 10.

Ingredients

7 chuck steaks

2 1 lbs. packages of polish sausages—sliced up

6 potatoes—cut up into chunks

4 carrots—cut into chunks

15 sliced-up mushrooms

1 onion—cut up into rings (like for onion rings)

2 tsp. of basil—cut up

1 tsp. of Italian seasoning

2 cobs on the corn—sliced up

7 pieces of foil cut into squares

1/2 cup of hoisin with garlic

Goulash

Directions

Cook the hamburger and onions, basil, Italian seasoning, chopped oregano, and garlic. Drain off oil from hamburger.

Add tomato sauce, and paste and diced tomatoes, sugar, cook for several hours. Macaroni noodles I cook in water and butter when they are done drain and put in a bowl add 4 tbs. butter and handful of basil chopped up fine.

Use the same sauce to make spaghetti. Add noodles in large bowl and mix the noodle with the sauce.

Serves 8.

Ingredients

1 lbs. hamburger

1 onion

4 tsp. fresh basil—chopped

1 tbs. Italian seasoning

1 6-oz. can tomato paste

2 tsp. of oregano—fresh

1/2 cup sugar

2 cloves of garlic—finely chopped

2 16-oz. cans of tomato sauce

1 14-oz. can diced tomatoes

Hamburger Gravy

Directions

Brown the onions, mushrooms, basil, oregano, all together and set a side.

Brown the hamburger in the same pan as all the spices and onion it will pick up the flavor. Add the beef stock and beef paste to the hamburger after its done and drained.

Now take some of the stock add to the 3 tbs. of flour and mix well in the bowl. Add this to the beef stock to thicken up the gravy. Cook this on medium heat until its thick. Add the mushrooms and onion mix to the gravy. Save some back to use a topping. Serve over mashed potatoes and top with mushrooms and onions and basil.

Serves 8.

Ingredients

1 2-lbs. package of hamburger

1 onion—chopped

1 tsp. of basil—chopped

1 tsp. of oregano

1 32-oz. can of beef stock

1 container of mushrooms—sliced

1 tsp. of Italian spice

Salt and pepper to taste

2 tsp. of beef paste

3 tbs. of flour mixed with a cup of beef broth

Hamburger Stew

Directions

Cook the hamburger, onions, carrots, celery, basil, Italian seasoning, garlic let this cook until done. Now add tomato sauce, paste, and stewed tomatoes. Now add beef stock and take a spoon and stir. Add polish sausage and chopped-up potatoes turn the heat on med heat on the stove. Now add the oregano and thyme to the pot and let cook for about 30 minutes. Add in the broccoli mixed vegetables. Cook for another 6 minutes and serve.

Serves 10.

Ingredients

2 lbs. of hamburger

8 carrots—sliced up

3 stocks of celery—cut up

2 tsp. basil—cut up

1 tsp. of Italian seasoning

2 cloves of garlic—chopped

7 potatoes—peeled and chopped

1 15-oz. can tomato sauce

1 15-oz can of whole tomatoes

1 6-oz. can of tomato paste

1 13-oz. package polish sausage—cut into chunks

1 12-oz. bag broccoli and mixed vegetables

1 onion—chopped

2 tsp. oregano—cut up

2 32-oz. container of beef stock

Hamburger Tortilla Salad

Directions

Fry up the hamburger Italian seasoning and onion together drain and set aside. Cut up the 2 tsp. of basil, 1 avocado, 3 tomatoes, 3 cups of lettuce, 2 carrots, 1 tsp. of thyme, 1 tsp. of oregano and salt and pepper to taste. Mix all together and add the hamburger that has time to drain. Put into a bowl and add the tortilla strips to the top of the salad.

Dressing: 1/4 cup of ranch dressing and 2 tsp. of honey and put over the top of the salad.

Serves 6.

Ingredients

1/2 lbs. of hamburger

3 tomatoes—chopped

1 tsp. of Italian seasoning

2 tsp. of fresh basil—cut up

1/2 an onion—finely chopped

1 avocado—peeled and cut up (optional)

3 cups of lettuce—cut up (or salad mix)

2 carrots—sliced

1 tsp. of thyme-freshly cut up

1 tsp. of oregano—cut up

Salt and pepper to your taste

1 cup of tortilla strips

1/4 cup of ranch dressing

2 tsp. of honey

Irish Corned Beef

Directions

In a roaster, put the corn beef, the beef stock, 1 tbs. of Italian spice, 1 tsp. of garlic, package of seasoning that the brisket came with, beef paste. When everything is in the roaster, pour the 1 oz. of Irish whiskey over the top of the meat and cook for 3 hours.

Then open the roaster and add the carrots, both kinds of cabbage, very small bag of red potatoes 2 lbs. cook for another hour or until potatoes and carrots are done.

Serves 8.

Ingredients

1 corned beef brisket

2 32-oz. cans of beef stock

1 tbs. of Italian spice

1 tsp. of garlic

1 oz. of Irish whiskey—poured on top of the brisket

The package of seasoning the brisket comes with—poured over the top

1/2 cabbage shredded up

1/2 of purple cabbage shredded up

6 carrots—cut up

1 lbs. of red potatoes

1 tbs. beef paste

Meatball Sub

Ingredients

Meatballs

2 pounds of hamburger

2 eggs

2 slices of bread—torn into chunks

2 tsp. of basil—chopped

2 tsp. of Italian seasoning

2 tsp. of oregano

1 onion—chopped

Directions

Form into balls. Use a small ice cream scoop, which forms the ball for you. Put the meatballs into a frying pan and fry until they are all browned. Take them out of the pan and set them aside.

Sauce

Ingredients

1 onion—chopped

4 tsp. fresh basil

1 tbs. Italian seasoning

1 6-oz. can tomato paste

2 tsp. of oregano—fresh

1/2 cup sugar

2 cloves of garlic—finely chopped

2 15-oz. cans of tomato sauce

Directions

You are going to cook all the ingredients for the sauce for about 10 minutes.

Take the meatballs and sauce put them together to cook in pan for about 35 minutes on top of the stove on med heat. You want the sauce to get into the meat.

Sandwich

Ingredients

8 hoagie rolls

Directions

Add the meatballs and sauce into the hoagie roll and sprinkle with cheese and serve.

Serves 8.

Meatloaf

BBQ Sauce

Ingredients

1/2 cup honey BBQ sauce

2 tbs. of honey

2 tsp. of hoisin sauce

1/4 cup sugar

1 tsp. of teriyaki sauce

Directions

Mix the sauce all together and spread it over the meatloaf for another 15 minutes and serve.

Serves 8.

Ingredients

2 pounds of hamburger

One onion—chopped

3 eggs

2 pieces of bread—torn up

1 tsp. of basil—chopped

1 tsp. Italian seasoning

1 tsp. oregano

1 tbs. honey-flavored BBQ sauce in the meatloaf

Directions

Mix all together with your hands and place on baking dish. Bake at 350 for about 45 minutes. Add sauce before baking.

Mongolian Beef and Broccoli

Ingredients

2 lbs. of chuck steak—cut up

2 tbs. of hoisin sauce

1 tbs. of chopped-up garlic

1/2 c soy sauce

1/2 cup water

6 tbs. of brown sugar

2 tbs. of flour

2 onions—chopped

1 tbs. of basil

2 tbs. of oregano

1 tbs. of olive oil

2 cups sliced up mushrooms

3 cups of broccoli—cooked for about less than
5 minutes so they still have a crunch to them.
Set aside

Directions

Chuck steaks cut into chunks and add basil, oregano, thyme, onion diced up and olive oil into a big bowl mix up and let set into the herbs in the fridge until you're ready to cook them.

Cook the chopped meat in 2 tbs. of olive and butter, basil, thyme until almost done so no more than 4 minutes on both sides. Then add the mushrooms and cook those for a few minutes.

Now cook the sauce.

Add the hoisin sauce, brown sugar, and garlic to a pan. Cook for a few minutes. Add a chopped-up onion to the pan and cook for a few more minutes, add the soy sauce, and water to the pan. Add in the flour mixed with a little water (2 tbs.) so the sauce thickens.

Take the cooked broccoli add to the sauce along with the meat mixture and cook for another 15 minutes. Cook over medium heat as you don't want the sauce to burn.

Serve over noodles.

Serves 10.

Polish Sausage Stir-Fry

Directions

Precook baby corn, polish sausage, carrots, all together for 5 minutes. Drain and set aside.

Cook mushrooms and chopped-up onions together in a tsp. of olive oil for 2 minutes.

Sauce: 4 tbs. of butter, 2 cloves of chopped-up garlic, 1 tsp. of oregano, 2 tsp. of thyme, basil, hoisin sauce. Mix together and heat up the mixture in the microwave for 1 minute.

Mix all ingredients together in a big bowl add precooked potatoes and corn, and polish sausage to the bowl.

Pour sauce over the top. Mix well and serve.

Serves 8–10.

Ingredients

1 cup baby corn oriental veggies (broccoli, baby corn)

6 Polish sausages—cut into slices

4 carrots—sliced

1 chopped onion

15 mushrooms—sliced

Salt and pepper to taste

1 tsp. oregano

1 tsp. basil-fresh

2 tbs. of hoisin sauce

Short Ribs

Ingredients

10 short ribs

1 onion—chopped

2 stocks of celery—chopped

2 tsp. of thyme

1 tsp. of oregano

4 carrots cut up

1 tsp. Italian seasoning

1 tsp. basil—chopped

French Onion Soup

2 onions—chopped

1/2 stick of butter

2 containers of beef stock

1 tsp. of basil chopped finely

2 tsp. of thyme, 2 cloves of garlic, 2 tsp. of beef paste

Directions

Cook onions in the butter and olive oil now add basil, oregano together until onions are brown and tender. Add 2 containers of beef stock and beef paste let cook for about 2 hours. Cook on medium heat until done. Set aside.

Now that the french onion soup is made, it's time to make the short ribs.

Short Ribs

1 onion-chopped, 2 stocks of celery, 2 tsp. of thyme, 1 tsp. of oregano,4 carrots cut up,1 tsp. Italian seasoning,1 tsp. basil. Cook this in butter and olive oil until the onions are soft set aside.

In the same pan, add a little butter and brown the short ribs on all sides so they are nice and brown. I use a Dutch oven to make my short ribs. Place the short ribs at the bottom and cover them with french onion soup.

Add in the onion mixture to this over the top along with the chopped-up carrots. Put the lid on and bake this 350 for 4 hours. In 4 hours, this will fall apart. When this is done, take some of the juice and make a gravy and serve over top of short ribs.

Serves 8–10.

Sliced Beef Hoagie

Directions

In a frying pan, put a bit of butter and olive oil, add the onion, basil, thyme, then add the sliced roast beef and cook for 6 minutes just until the onions get tender. Don't overcook, as the sliced beef will get tough.

Time to build the subs.

Add your favorite sauce on both sides of the bread. I use ranch and honey mixed together gives the subs a tang. Add roast beef mixture.

Add chopped-up avocado and either sliced or chopped tomatoes. Add more onion if that is what you like. Sprinkle with cheese.

Serves 8.

Ingredients

2 lbs. sliced roast beef

1 tsp. of fresh basil—chopped

3. 1 onion—chopped

sub rolls, like a hoagie roll

1 small container of fresh mushrooms
(you might want to chop them smaller)

cheese—I usually just sprinkle on cheese
at the end

3 avocados

a pinch of thyme

chopped-up tomatoes to sprinkle over the top

Spaghetti

Directions

Cook the hamburger and onions, basil, Italian seasoning, and garlic. Drain.

Add tomato sauce, tomato paste and diced tomatoes, sugar, and oregano to hamburger mixture cook for several hours.

Spaghetti noodles I cook in water and butter when they are done drain and put in a bowl add 4 tbs. butter and handful of chopped-up basil. Now add spaghetti noodles to the plate add sauce on top with basil.

Serves 10-plus people.

Ingredients

1 lbs. hamburger

1 onion

4 tsp. basil—cut up

1 tbs. Italian seasoning

1 6-oz can tomato paste

2 tsp. of oregano—cut up

1/2 cup sugar

2 cloves of garlic cut up finely

2 15-oz. cans of tomato sauce

1 15-oz. can diced tomatoes

Taco Salad

Directions

Take the hamburger and turkey, 1 onion, Italian seasoning, basil, oregano, garlic. Now cook all these ingredients together. When they are done, drain off any of the grease that the hamburger created.

Salad

Take the shredded lettuce and lay down on a plate next take the meat mixture, then cut tomatoes, avocado, some chopped-up basil, and chopped-up onions. Top with a sprinkle of cheese.

Sauce

2 tbs. of ranch dressing, 2 tbs. of honey mix together pour over the top of the salad. Serve with garlic bread.

Serves 6.

Ingredients

1 16-oz. package ground turkey

1 lbs. hamburger

1 onion—chopped

1 tsp. of Italian seasoning

1 tsp. of basil—chopped

1 tsp. of oregano—chopped

2 cloves of garlic—chopped

2 tomatoes—chopped

2 avocados—cut up

1 small package of shredded lettuce

Sprinkle of cheese on top

2 tbs. of ranch dressing

1 tbs. of honey

Teriyaki Steak and Mushrooms

Directions

Mix all marinade together and pour over the top of the cut steaks that are in chunks. Add mushrooms together to marinate for a couple of hours or until dinner.

Now to fix dinner.

Take all the steaks mixture pour into a greased or sprayed baking dish. Mix up and bake for about 1 hour, or until the meat is tender and easy to cut with a fork.

Bake at 350 for about 1 hour.

Serve over the top of rice, noodles, or potatoes.

Serves 8.

Ingredients

4 steaks—cut up

1 package of mushrooms

Sauce to marinate the meat

1 tsp. of soy sauce

1 onion—diced

1 tsp. of basil—cut up

1 tsp. of Italian seasoning

1/4 cup of brown sugar

2 tbs. of hoisin sauce

1 tbs. of sesame seed oil

1 tsp. of thyme—dried

2 tbs. of pineapple juice

Turkey and Hamburger Hash

Directions

Cook of the above ingredients together in one big frying pan make sure to drain the meat mixture.

Add precooked potatoes to the meat mixture cook on medium heat for about 15 minutes.

Can be served by itself or with a taco shell or served with a bun.

Serves 6.

Ingredients

1 16-oz. package of ground turkey

1 lbs. of hamburger

1 tsp. of basil—chopped up (dried works to I have tried it both ways)

1 tsp. of thyme—chopped (fresh works better)

1 tsp. of rosemary—chopped

1 onion—chopped

2 cups precooked potatoes

Zesty Orange Meatballs

Sauce

Ingredients

1/2 cup orange juice

1 cup brown sugar

1 tbs. soy sauce

pinch of salt and pepper

1 tsp. ginger

2 cloves of garlic

2 tsp. sesame oil

2 tbs. of hoisin sauce

One small can of tomato sauce 6 oz

Zest an orange in sauce

1/2 cup bourbon BBQ sauce

Ingredients

2 pounds of hamburger

1 onion—chopped

3 eggs

2 slices of bread-torn up into small chunks

1 tsp. Italian seasoning

1 tsp. oregano

Directions

Mix all together and form into balls brown in a frying pan on both sides, then remove from the pan.

Directions

Mix up cook on top of the stove until it just starts to boil.

Now take a 13 × 8 baking dish spray cooking spray, then add the meatballs and sauce over the top of the meatballs. Slice up the orange that you zested add the on top of the sauce. Bake at 350 for 30 minutes and serve over noodles or rice.

Serves 8.

Chicken

BBQ Chicken

BBQ Sauce

Ingredients

1/2 cup honey BBQ sauce

1/2 cup of brown sugar

2 tbs. of white Karo syrup

2 tbs. of hoisin sauce

1 tsp. soy sauce

1/2 tsp. of sesame seed oil (a very little goes a long way)

Directions

Cook for five minutes until sauce is combined. Than add over the top of the chicken half way through cooking time. Making sure to keep turning the chicken.

Ingredients

10 pieces of chicken I used thighs

1 tsp. poultry seasoning

1 onion—chopped

1 tsp. basil—cut up

1 tsp. rosemary—cut up

1 tsp. of olive oil

Directions

Take the chicken marinate it in the poultry seasoning, onion, basil, rosemary and olive oil. Set in the fridge for about 1 hour. Place on sprayed cookie sheet and bake at 350 degrees for 45–55 minutes. Make sure halfway through you put BBQ sauce on to finish the cooking. Turn at least once during the cooking.

Serves 8.

Cinnamon Crunch Chicken

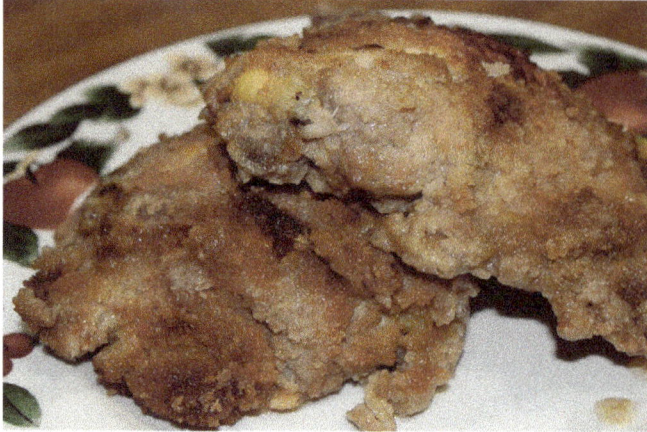

Ingredients

12 legs and thighs chicken (choose the chicken you like)

4 eggs

2 cups of milk

1 tsp. of cinnamon

1/4 cup of sugar

Directions

32-oz. bag Cinnamon Toast Crunch cereal—use a processor; it will be easier to turn this cereal to dust. If you don't have a processor, then put cereal into a plastic bag and seal it up and use a rolling pin to roll into dust.

Marinade

Basil 4 (tsp.), 1 onion. Marinate chicken in this for at least 1 hour so all the flavors marry together and soak into the chicken. Put in the fridge until time to make dinner.

Mix egg, milk, cinnamon, and sugar. Dip chicken in egg mixture, then roll in crushed cinnamon crunch cereal. Coat until covered. Place coated chicken on a sprayed sheet pan and bake for 55 minutes. Cook at 350 degrees. Make sure to turn the chicken during cooking.

Serves 10.

Chicken and Dumplings

Dumplings

Ingredients

2 cups of baking mix (like Bisquick)

2/3 cup of milk

Directions

Mix together, the dough will be sticky so just spoon into the chicken mixture. Let the dumplings cook for 10 minutes in a covered pot, then another 10 minutes without the lid. By the time the dumplings are done, the chicken mixture will be nice and thick. It would have made its own gravy.

Serves 10.

Ingredients

12 pieces of chicken

4 stocks of celery—cut up

5 carrots—sliced up

1 onion cut up

2 32-oz. chicken broth containers

1 tsp. of basil—cut up

1 tsp. Poultry seasoning

12-oz. package of broccoli

Directions

Put all the chicken you want to use in a big pot with the ingredients above except the carrots and broccoli. Let cook for about 3 hours, or until chicken is done. Cook over medium heat on top of the stove with a lid.

When chicken is done, take out of the pot and cut it up after it cools, then add the chicken back into the chicken stock. Add the broccoli, carrots, and cook with the chicken until the carrots are tender.

You can either make homemade dumplings or use biscuit mix.

Chicken and Bacon Mac and Cheese

Ingredients

8 chicken breasts

4 cups of macaroni

1 1-lbs. package of bacon—maple flavored is what I used

1 onion—chopped

2 tsp. fresh basil—chopped (dried can be used to)

1 tsp. poultry seasoning

1 tsp. fresh oregano—chopped

2 cups of pepper jack cheese—shredded

1 1/2 cup of cheddar cheese—shredded

3 tsp. of powder ranch dressing

3 cups of milk

Directions

Cook the 4 cups of macaroni and set aside. Put a little butter in the macaroni to keep it from sticking together.

Put cut up chicken with the basil, onion, oregano, and poultry seasoning. Mix together and set inside the fridge. This way, it gets all the flavors into the chicken.

Next, cook the bacon and chop it up into chucks. Set it aside.

Take the chicken and all the herbs and cook it in the same pan as the bacon until tender.

Drain all bacon drippings out of the pan. Put 3 tbs. of butter in the pan and add 3 tbs. of flour to make a rue. Mix it up until there are no lumps. Now add the 3 cups of milk and stir with a whisk until smooth.

Add the pepper jack cheese to the sauce and the cheddar cheese and stir until the sauce has melted all the cheese. Cook this over medium heat. Stir this all the time so it doesn't burn.

Add the 3 tsp. of powder ranch dressing to the sauce and stir and take it off the heat.

Put the macaroni in greased baking dish. Add the chicken and mix up. Add all the sauce and stir up.

Over the top of mac and cheese, you will sprinkle over the bacon all over the top of the mac and cheese.

Bake a 350 for about 10 minutes.

Serves 10.

Chicken Broccoli Salad

Directions

Chicken

Boil the chicken in the chicken stock, poultry seasoning, basil, 1 cut up onion, until tender. After it is done and cooled to touch cut it up into chucks and set aside. The stock put into the freezer to use a later date.

Cook the pasta until done drain now add to big bowl and add butter about 1 tbs. and mix up.

Add the chicken that is cut up into chucks, 1 tsp. of oregano, and 1 can sliced black olives.

Cut up cooked broccoli that is cooled so you can cut it up. Add this to the bowl with the 1 tsp. of Italian seasoning and the basil.

Add a container of mushrooms that are sliced up. Grate the 3 carrots and put this into the bowl.

For this onion slice up a red onion, add 3 tbs. of package ranch dressing. Mix all of this together with the mayo. Next add 1 tsp. of garlic powder. Now add the bacon chucks on top of the salad put it in the fridge for about 1 hour and let all these flavors marry together.

Use your favor salad dressing.

Serves 10.

Ingredients

3 cups of cut up chicken

2 tsp. of fresh basil cut up

2 onions—cut up in small chunks

4 cups of pasta

1 3-oz. can sliced black olives—drained

2 cups of cherry tomatoes—yellow and red cut into half

2 cups of broccoli—cut up

1 lbs. package of maple-flavored bacon—fried and cut up into chunks

1 tsp. Italian seasoning

2 avocados—cut up (optional)

1 15 mushrooms—slice up (optional)

3 carrots—grated

3 tbs. of ranch dressing—package

2 32-oz. containers chicken stock

2 tsp. of poultry seasoning

1 tsp. of garlic powder

Chicken Marinara Burrito

Ingredients

1 32-oz. jar marinara sauce

2 onions

3 cups chicken—chopped into small pieces

4 tsp. oregano—chopped

4 tsp. basil—chopped

4 tsp. Italian seasoning

1 tsp. poultry seasoning

3 tsp. butter

3 tbs. olive oil

1 package of spaghetti sauce

2 tbs. of sugar

3 cups of grated cheese—cheddar

10 burrito shells—floured

1 can sliced black olives 4 oz. (optional)

Directions

Sauce for over the top: 1 32-oz. jar of marinara sauce pour into a sauce pan next add the 2 tsp. of chopped-up oregano, add the one package of spaghetti sauce mix, sugar, 2 tsp. of Italian seasoning mix all together and let simmer for about 15 minutes. Set aside.

Chicken

Cook 3 cups of cut-up chicken with two onions, 2 tsp. of basil, 2 tsp. of oregano, 2 tsp. of Italian, 1 tsp. of poultry seasoning, 3 tsp. of olive oil, 3 tsp. of butter. Mix all together and fry up chicken until done, which is less than 5 minutes. When done, drain and put into a bowl. Set aside.

Take the marinara sauce you doctored up and put some down on the 3 × 9-inch baking dish. Take one of the burritos shells fill with chicken mixture and sprinkle with the grated cheese. Now fold it up and put it face down on the sauce. Continue until you get all the shells filled up. Place face down on the sauce.

Now cover with the sauce, then add cheese over the top and bake in the oven for about 15 minutes at 350.

Serves 10.

Chicken Parmesan

Spaghetti Sauce

Ingredients

1 onion—diced up

4 tsp. basil—chopped

1 tbs. Italian seasoning

2 tsp. of fresh oregano—chopped or dried oregano works too

1/2 cup sugar

2 cloves of garlic cut up

1 16-oz. can of tomato sauce

Directions

Mix all the sauce ingredients together and cook on the stove for at least 30 minutes so you can get all the flavors to merry together.

Now take a baking dish that is 13×9 and spray the pan with cooking spray. Place the chicken in the dish. Pour the sauce over the top of the chicken and cook for 55 minutes. Bake at 350 the last 10 minutes of cooking add cheddar cheese over the top. Serve over noodles that have butter, basil, and oregano.

Serves 8.

Ingredients

Mix for chicken

12 pieces of chicken (adjust to what you are going to need)

1 tsp. basil

1 onion chopped

1 tsp. poultry seasoning

1 tsp. Italian seasoning

1 tsp. of olive oil

Directions

Now take the chicken with all the ingredients above and mix together and set in the fridge until you get ready to make dinner, or for about 1 hour to have the herbs to get into the meat.

Place in chicken in an egg wash. Mix this up. Dip the chicken into the egg wash, then coat the chicken in flour. put chicken into a frying skillet with a little vegetable oil and brown on both sides. Take the chicken out and set aside until you get the sauce done.

Now take this out of the pan and set aside as it is not done yet. I use my spaghetti sauce to put over the top.

Chicken pot pie

Ingredients

Filling for pot pie

3 cups shredded chicken – get roasted chicken from the store

2 peeled potatoes – cut into chucks – pre-cook potatoes for about 6 minutes

1 cup carrots – cut up into small chunks

1 cup peas or use the veggies you like

1 cup celery – cut up

1 onion – diced up

3 tbsp of butter

1 package chicken gravy

1 package pie dough – set this out for about an hour before using

4 tbsp. flour

1 tsp thyme – cut up

1 tsp rosemary – cut up

1 container chicken stock

Directions

Shred chicken set aside

Put butter in the frying pan than add the chopped-up onion, then carrots, celery, thyme, rosemary cook until tender.

Now add the flour to this mixture of veggies cook until you can't see the flour anymore, so it doesn't have a flour taste to it.

Stir this until it makes a rue now add in 2 cups of chicken stock.

Now add in potatoes- pre-cook potatoes than set aside after they are drained.

Add in the chicken gravy package this will add in flavor- if you find the filling is to thick add big spoonful of chicken stock.

Now add in the cut-up chicken and stir. Now filling is made set aside.

Pie tins

Roll out the pie dough that has been setting out make sure it is bigger than the pie tin.

Take rolling pin roll up the pie dough on to it than roll out on top of pie tin. Making sure to drape the pie dough inside and extra pie dough around the edge fold under the edge.

Take a fork and poke little holes into the shell.

Now add in the chicken pot pie filling 3/4 the way to the top.

Next roll out the top crust over the top of the filling.

Pinch together pie dough along the edge so filling doesn't come out. Then take pinch your fingers together along the edge of the pie until you have fluted edge. Or you can use a fork to go along the edge that works to.

Put foil around the edge of pie so it doesn't burn halfway through baking remove the foil to finish baking. Brush the pie with an egg wash- 1 egg and couple tablespoons of water mix up. Brush on to the top of the pie.

Bake at 350 for 35 to 40 minutes when the crust is brown it will be done.

Serves 6.

Chicken Stew

Directions

Boil the chicken in the chicken stock, chopped-up onion, 1 tsp. of basil, rosemary, garlic, poultry seasoning, celery cut up. For about 55 minutes or until done. Now take the chicken out of the juice. Put it in the fridge until its cool enough to touch, then cut it up.

Add chicken back to the stock along with all the potatoes cut up, carrots cut up, chopped-up basil, and garlic cut into pieces. I also use California blend veggies that I put in at the last 30 minutes of cooking. Cook on the stove for about 45 minutes or until veggies and potatoes are done.

Serves 8.

Ingredients

8 chicken thighs

7 carrots—cut up

1 tsp. rosemary—finely chopped

4 potatoes—cut up

1 tsp. of basil—freshly cut up

Garlic 2 cloves cut up or 1/4 tsp. of garlic powder

celery 4 stalks cut up

2 32-oz. containers of chicken stock

California blend vegs one small bag-broccoli mix vegs 12 oz

1 tsp. poultry seasoning

1 onion—cut up

1 red bell pepper—cut up and seeds taken out

Chicken Stir-Fry

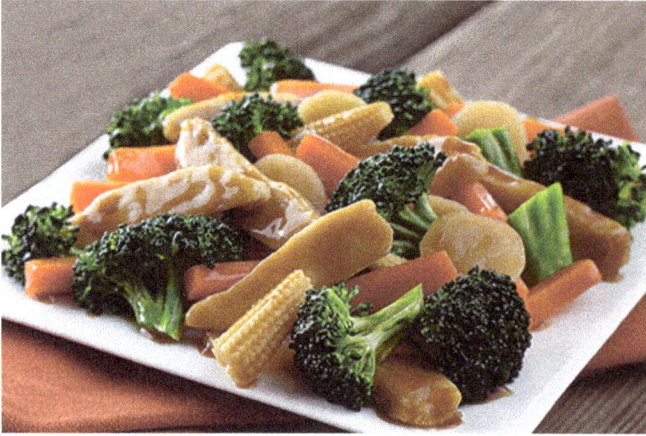

Directions

Precook carrots, broccoli, for about five minutes in boiling water you still want the vegs not done all the way. Then set aside.

Now cook the chicken in the onions, thyme, olive oil, butter, Italian seasoning, oregano, garlic, basil. Make sure to cut up the chicken breast into either strips or chunks as I did. This should take about 10 minutes. Set aside.

Now in the pan you cooked the chicken in add 1 cup brown sugar,1 tbs. soy sauce, Salt and pepper to taste,1 tsp. ginger, 1/2 cup sesame oil, 2 tbs. of hoisin sauce mixes all together.

Add in the all the veggies, including the baby corn, the chicken mixture, and mix all together.

You can either serve over noodles or serve it right to the plate with garlic bread.

Serves 8.

Ingredients

1 cup brown sugar

1 tbs. soy sauce

Salt and pepper to taste

1 tsp. ginger

2 cloves of garlic

1/2 cup sesame oil

2 tbs. of hoisin sauce

2 cups of broccoli—cut up

1 cup of baby corn—canned will work

6 carrots—cut up

1 onion—cut up into small pieces

1 tsp. of Italian seasoning

1 tsp. of basil—cut up or dried

1 tsp. of oregano–cut up

1 tsp. of thyme—cut up

6 pieces of chicken breasts—cut up and fried in butter and olive oil

2 tbs. of butter

2 tbs. of olive oil

Fried Chicken

Ingredients

8 pieces of chicken

3 eggs

1 cup of milk

2 tsp. of poultry seasoning

3 cups of flour

2 tsp. of dried basil

Marinade for Chicken

1 tsp. poultry seasoning, one onion diced up, 1 tsp. thyme cut up, 1 tsp. chicken bouillon paste, 1 tbs. olive oil. Mix all together. Add to chicken and put into the fridge for about 30 minutes. When you're ready to fry the chicken, take it out and start the next part of the recipe.

Directions

In a bowl, add the eggs, milk, 1 tsp. of poultry seasoning, 1 tsp. of dried basil and mix all together and set aside.

In the flour, add a 1 tsp. of basil, 1 tsp. of poultry seasoning mix together. I set things up egg mixture in a bowl to dip the chicken in and dip into the flour, then into the frying pan to brown the chicken on both sides until golden brown. Then take the chicken and put it on to a baking dish because now it goes into the oven for 35 minutes at 350.

Serves 8.

Hawaiian Chicken Wings

Ingredients

3 packages of wings

1 onion—chopped

3 tbs. of fresh basil—chopped

1 tbs. soy sauce

1 cup brown sugar

3 tbs. hoisin sauce

1/2 tsp. of garlic powder

1 16-oz. can pineapple chunks-drained

1 lbs. of maple-flavored bacon—fried and chopped

2 tbs. BBQs sauce

1/4 cup of corn syrup

Directions

Put wings in a big bowl early in the day. with the 3 tbs. of basil, 1 chopped-up onion. Add two tbs. of olive oil now mix all together and let sit in the fridge for a couple of hours.

Sauce

Soy sauce, brown sugar, hoisin sauce, garlic powder, can of pineapple chunks, 2 tbs. BBQ sauce, and corn syrup. Zest 3 oranges in the sauce cook the sauce on the stove for a few minutes. Set aside.

Slice up the oranges you zested earlier and set aside. They will be layered into the wings.

Take the wings out of the fridge because you are going to layer everything together. Put a spoonful of sauce on the bottom of the baking dish, then a layer of wings, then chopped-up bacon, then sauce, and finally sliced halo oranges. Repeat this process until the pan is full.

Bake at 350 for 2 hours. Serve over rice and garnish with the chopped-up bacon.

Serves 8.

Lemon Chicken

Directions

Take the cube of butter and the lemon zest and garlic pepper and mix together set it aside.

Now take the chicken and pat it dry so the lemon butter will stay on the chicken while it bakes. Add lemon butter over the top of the chicken and put it in a 13 × 9 baking dish.

Add cut-up bacon, broccoli, and carrots around the side of the chicken. Top with the sliced-up lemons over the top of the chicken and bake 45 minutes. 350 degrees.

Serves 8.

Ingredients

8 pieces of chicken

Note: Chicken was marinated in 1 tsp. of basil, 1 chopped-up onion, 1 tsp. of fresh rosemary, 1 tsp. of poultry seasoning for about 1 hour. Place in the fridge.

7 carrots—chopped

3 cups of broccoli—cut up (you can use frozen if that's easier)

1 onion (chopped)

1 lbs. package of bacon—fried and cut into pieces

2 lemons—sliced up

1 cube of butter

2 lemons—zested

1 tsp. of garlic pepper

Orange Chicken

Directions

Mix up sauce 1/2 cup orange juice, 1 cup brown sugar, 1 tsp. soy sauce, ginger, 1 tsp. sesame seed oil. Mix up and add chicken to sauce. 1/2 can of pineapple chucks, add sliced oranges to the sauce. Now add the sauce over the top of the chicken and cook for 45 minutes at 350 degrees. Serve over rice.

Serves 8.

Ingredients

10 chicken thighs and legs—cut up

1/2 cup orange juice

1 cup brown sugar

1 tbs. soy sauce

Salt and pepper

1 tsp. ginger

2 cloves of garlic—finely chopped

1 tsp. sesame oil

2 tbs. of hoisin sauce

1/2 can 20-oz. pineapple

Zest one orange—slice the orange and put into the sauce

Soak the chicken in a handful of basil, one onion chopped up, salt, and pepper. Soak chicken for a couple hours before baking. Put into the fridge

Roasted Chicken

Directions

Chop up fine the rosemary, add in the poultry seasoning, add chopped-up carrots and onions, celery, and basil. Cook in the olive oil and butter so all the favors marry together. Put chicken in roasting pan with all the veggies and onions, butter, olive oil. Pour chicken stock and veggies in pan over the top of chicken. Cook the chicken in the oven at 350 degrees for about 2 hours or until done.

Serves 10.

Put the stock in the freezer for use later for another recipe.

Ingredients

1 whole chicken

1 tsp. rosemary

4 tsp. of butter

2 tsp. poultry seasoning

2 32-oz. containers of chicken stock

7 carrots

2 onions

4 stocks of celery

A splash of olive oil

1 tsp. of basil

Soft Chicken Taco

Taco

Ingredients

4 tomatoes—cut up

1/4 of head of lettuce—chopped up

3 avocados cut up

1 tsp. basil—cut up

1 package of tortilla shells

Directions

Chop up ingredients and put into separate little bowls.

Lay the shell over a plate and start building the soft taco put the lettuce down, then chicken, avocado, tomato, cheese, a little bit more chicken. Sprinkle Italian seasoning over the top with your favorite dressing.

Serves 10.

Ingredients

10 pieces of chicken

1 tsp. of basil—chopped

1 onion—chopped up

1 tsp. of poultry seasoning

Directions

Mix up the chicken, basil, 1 onion, poultry seasoning in big bowl put into the fridge for about 1 hour.

2 32-oz. containers of chicken stock.

1 tsp. of poultry seasoning.

Put into a big pot add chicken and chicken stock.

1 tsp. of poultry season and cook until done.

When the chicken is cool enough to touch, cut it up into chunks and set aside. Put stock into freezer for another recipe.

Sweet and Sour Chicken

Directions

Put chicken in chicken stock, poultry seasoning, and basil. Cook all together until the chicken is done. Put chicken stock in the freezer and save until another time to use.

Take chicken and cut into pieces add the sauce over the chicken. Cook on stove top for a about 10 minutes to let all the flavors marry together. Take the sweet and sour chicken and put over rice and serve it.

Serves 10.

Ingredients

8 chicken thighs (no bones)

2 32-oz. chicken stock

2 tsp. of poultry seasoning

2 tbs. fresh basil—chopped

Sauce

2 tsp. of soy sauce

1/2 cup ketchup

1/2 cup sugar

2 tbs. vinegar

1 tsp. hoisin sauce

Mix together for the sauce; cook for a few minutes

Chickelia Skillet

Directions

Place chorizo, veggies and ham in a large skillet on medium heat until chorizo is cooked.

In a blender place soften chilies, garlic and a pinch of salt with a cup of water to blend. Strain as you put it into the skillet.

Stir until all the ingredients are stirred in, then let it cool. Sprinkle with cheese and serve tortilla chips.

Serves 8.

Ingredients

1 rotisserie chicken (shredded)

2 15-oz. cans of mixed veggies

1 6-oz. package of chorizo

3 guajillo dried chili pepper—soak in a half cup of water until soft

1 clove of garlic—cut up

1 1/2 cups of diced ham

1 bag of tortilla chips

2 cups of shredded cheese

Seafood
Fish
and
Shrimp

Ceviche

Directions

Take everything from above and mix into a big bowl and mix it all together serve with tortilla chips. If you like it spicy, then add hot sauce on top of what you put onto your plate.

Serves 10.

Ingredients

5 pounds of shrimp put into a bowl

3 lbs. small package of Imitation crab—all cut up

5 cucumbers peeled, and seeds taken out—cut up

5 carrots shredded

15 radishes—shredded

7 oz. of cilantro—finely chopped

2 limes—juiced into the bowl; put over the top and mixed in

6 tomatoes—cut up

2 onions—diced up

Buttered Garlic Fish

Directions

Sauce

Cook 3 stocks of finely chopped celery and onion. Cook for a few minutes. Take them out and set them aside. In a small bowl, add 2 cubes of melted butter, 2 cloves of garlic chopped up fine, 3 tbs. of basil chopped up, 1 tsp. dried oregano, 1 tsp. of Italian seasoning mix all together. Add in onions and celery to the butter. Stir it all together. This is the sauce you will pour over the fish.

Add a spoonful of sauce to the bottom of the baking dish. Layer fillets, then butter sauce over the top of the fish until the baking dish is full. Add the last bit of sauce over the top of the fillets. Bake at 350 for 1 hour, as the fillets are small and cook quick.

Serves 8.

Ingredients

1 package of tilapia fillets

3 stocks of celery—finely chopped

2 cubes of butter—melted

2 cloves of garlic—finely chopped

3 tbs. of fresh basil—finely chopped

1 tsp. of dried oregano

1 onion—finely chopped

1 tsp. Italian seasoning

Fried Fish

Ingredients

8 slices of cod

3 eggs—for egg wash

2 cups of flour

2 cups of panko breadcrumbs

1 tsp. Italian seasoning

1 tsp. old bay garlic and herb seasoning

1 lemon—juiced on fish after it's done

Directions

You are going to set up 3 stations: first, flour mixture; second, egg wash; third, panko breadcrumbs.

Dip the fish into the flour mixture, then into the egg mixture. Dip into the panko bread mixture. Add enough oil to the bottom of the frying to cover the bottom of the pan.

When the pan is hot enough, add in coated fish. You will have to babysit the fish, as it will brown fast. Once it has brown on one side flip to the other side once both sides are brown put in oven to keep warm until all the fish is done.

It will be crunchy on the outside and tender on the inside.

Just before serving, juice one lemon over the fish.

Serves 6.

Lemon Shrimp

Directions

Add butter, olive oil, and garlic to the pan. Add in shrimp. Cook until pink. Cook this on medium heat for a few minutes until the shrimp turns pink.

Zest a whole lemon, then juice the lemon in the frying pan. Add in the chicken bouillon paste stir. Let cook for another five minutes.

Serve with a salad and garlic toast.

Serves 6.

Ingredients

3 cups of shrimp—when the shrimp turns pink, take them out (make sure to get deveined shrimp)

1 cube of butter—use real butter

5 cloves of garlic—peeled and cut up

1 lemon—zested and juiced

1 tsp. chicken bouillon paste

4 tbs. of olive oil

Shrimp and Broccoli Scampi

Directions

Add butter, olive oil, and garlic to the pan. Add in shrimp. Cook until pink.

Zest a whole lemon, then juice the lemon in the pan. Add in the chicken bouillon paste and stir.

Add in the broccoli to the shrimp. Cook for a few minutes.

The noodles are now done. Add in the noodles, one spoonful at a time, until both cups of noodles are added.

Add cheese in and stir the mixture.

Stir shrimp mixture and noodles together and serve in bowl or plate.

Serves 6.

Ingredients

3 cups of shrimp—when the shrimp turns pink take them out

1 cube of butter

4 cloves of garlic—peeled and cut up

1 lemon—zested and juiced

1 cup of broccoli—cut up smaller

2 cups of noodles

1 tsp. chicken bullion

4 tbs. of olive oil

1/2 cup grated cheese—added at the end

Shrimp Stir-Fry

Directions

Add to frying pan the butter, garlic, onion, mushrooms, rosemary, chicken gravy, and fry until mushrooms are tender.

Next, add in the precooked shrimp and stir. Let cook until shrimp is hot, then serve over butter noodles. Now take the basil and use for garnish.

Serves 8.

Ingredients

2 pounds of shrimp-jumbo shrimp—precooked

4 cloves Elephant garlic—peeled and cut up

2 tsp. basil—cut up

2 cups mushrooms—sliced up

1 onion cut up

4 tbs. of butter

1 tsp. of rosemary-freshly cut up

1/2 package of chicken gravy

3 cups of noodles—cooked and drained
set aside

Pork

BBQ Country Pork Ribs

BBQ Sauce

Ingredients

1/2 cup honey BBQ sauce

1/2 cup of brown sugar

2 tbs. of molasses

2 tbs. of hoisin sauce

1 tsp. soy sauce

1/2 tsp. of sesame seed oil (a very little goes a long way)

Directions

Mix this all together, then add this to a saucepan and cook 1–2 minutes so all ingredients marry together. Here's the fun part: Now you are going to add this wonderful BBQ sauce over the ribs the ribs that have been cooking in beef broth for the last several hours. Cook for another 45 minutes so that all the BBQ sauce has gone done into piece of the meat. Bake at 350 for a total of 3 hours.

Serves 8.

Ingredients

10 pork country ribs

1 tsp. of basil—cut up

1 tsp. of thyme

2 chopped up onion

1 tsp. of Italian seasoning

2 32-oz. containers of beef broth

Directions

Take the ribs and marinate them in the basil, thyme, onion, Italian seasoning, and garlic for about 1 hour in the fridge. The meat will soak all the flavor in these herbs.

Now take the ribs all the herbs they have been soaking and put into roasting pan. Add the two containers of beef broth to the roasting pan. Bake at 350 for 2 hours. Drain all juice from pan after the 2 hours.

BBQ Pork Steaks

BBQ Sauce

Ingredients

1/2 cup honey BBQ sauce

2 tsp. of hoisin sauce

1/2 cup brown sugar

1 tsp. soy sauce

2 drops of sesame seed oil (a little goes a long way)

Directions

Mix BBQ sauce, hoisin sauce, brown sugar, 1 tsp. soy sauce, and sesame seed oil. Mix all together.

Take the pork steaks that has been in the fridge soaking in all those herbs. Put the pork steaks on a sprayed pan place them on the cookie sheet or baking dish.

Cover the pork steaks in the BBQ sauce you just made bake them at 350 for 55 minutes. Halfway through the baking check the pork steaks if it has lots of juice empty the pan of the juice. Add more BBQ sauce the last little bit of baking.

Serves 8.

Ingredients

Marinade for Pork Steaks

8 pork steaks

2 tsp. of basil—cut up

2 tsp. of thyme—cut up

1 onion—chopped up

1/2 tsp. of garlic

2 tsp. of olive oil

Directions

Mix all the pork steaks, basil, thyme, onion, garlic, and olive oil. Coat the meat and let it set in the fridge until you get ready to put it in the oven.

Country Ribs and Gravy

Directions

Take the ribs and marinate them in the basil, thyme, and onion, Italian seasoning and garlic for about 1 hour in the fridge. The meat will soak all the flavor in these herbs. Now take the country ribs and put them into a deep baking dish to bake, like a Dutch oven or a roasting pan.

Add the two containers of beef broth, the carrots, onion (chopped) over the top of the ribs to cook for 3 hours so they are tender to cut with a fork or eat off the bone.

Now to make the gravy.

Take the 4 tbs. of butter and melt into a saucepan add the flour to the butter so it makes a rue.

Add 2 cups broth from the country ribs to the rue using a whisk to stir with. Keep stirring as the gravy thickens. Now add a cup of milk to the gravy to smooth is out. Serve over the ribs. Add the carrots to the plate and serve.

Bake at 350 for 3 hours.

Serves 10.

Ingredients

10 country ribs (pork country ribs)

1 tsp. of basil—cut up

1 tsp. of thyme

2 chopped up onion

1 tsp. of Italian seasoning

2 32-oz. containers of beef broth

1/2 tsp. of garlic

4 carrots—cut up

4 tbs. of butter

4 tbs. of flour

Country Rib Salad

Directions

Take the ribs and marinate them in the basil, thyme, and onion, Italian seasoning and garlic for about 1 hour in the fridge. The meat will soak all the flavor in these herbs.

Now take the ribs all the herbs they have been soaking and put into roasting pan. Add the 2 containers of beef broth to the roasting pan. Bake for 3 hours.

Serves 10.

Ingredients

10 country ribs

1 tsp. of basil—cut up

1 tsp. of thyme

2 chopped-up onions

1 tsp. of Italian seasoning

2 32-oz. containers of beef broth

2 cups shredded lettuce or salad mix of your choice

1 cup of shredded carrots

1 tomato cut up

1/2 cup dried cranberries

1 avocado

Ham and Mushroom Burrito

Directions

Panfry the chopped-up ham, mushrooms, oregano, Italian seasoning, and dried basil together until mushrooms are cooked which is minutes.

Now brown the shells on the outside of the burrito shells.

Add the ham and mushroom mixture to the shells when they come out of the pan.

Add the chopped-up avocado and slice in half cherry tomatoes on top. Add ranch dressing on top—less than 1 tsp. You're only sprinkling over the top. Add the cheddar cheese over the top. Add the second shell that you browned and dig in.

Serves 1.

Ingredients

2 burrito shells—floured

10 sliced mushrooms

6 cherry tomatoes—sliced in half

1 avocado-cut up

1 tsp. of ranch dressing—packaged

1/2 tsp. of oregano

1/2 tsp. of Italian seasoning

1 tsp. of fresh basil—chopped up

1/2 tsp. of dried basil

1 tsp. of olive oil

1 tsp. of butter

2 slices of ham

2 tbs. of cheddar cheese

Pork Ribs

Ingredients

12 meaty pork ribs

1 tsp. of oregano

1 tsp. of basil

1 onion—diced up

1 tsp. of pure sesame seed oil (if you use too much, it will overpower the dish)

3 tbs. mandarin teriyaki sauce

2 tsp. of hoisin sauce

1 tsp. of garlic—dried

1/4 cup honey

1 tsp. soy sauce

1/4 cup chicken stock

Directions

Take all the ingredients above and put them in a bowl with the ribs. Put them into the fridge for about 1 hour.

When you're ready to bake the ribs put them in a Dutch oven is what I used. make sure to add all the juice over the ribs and bake them for about 2 hours or until tender. Just before they are done add 2 tbs. more mandarin teriyaki sauce over the top of the ribs bake another 10 minutes.

Bake at 350 for 2 hours take out of the oven and serve.

Serves 8.

Pork Roast

Ingredients

4 onions

1/2 stick of butter

2 32-oz. containers of beef stock

1 tsp. basil chopped finely

2 tsp. of thyme

2 cloves of garlic-cut up or ½ tsp. of dried garlic

2 tsp. of beef paste

Directions

Cook onions in the butter and olive oil.

Add basil, oregano, thyme together until onions are brown and tender.

Add 2 containers of beef stock and beef paste let cook for about two hours. Cook on medium heat until done, or for about 2 hours so all the flavors marry together (french onion soup).

Brown the pork roast on both sides in the same pan that you cooked the onions and herbs in. Put the roast into a roasting pan pour in the french onion soup over the roast cover with foil and cook for 5 hours. If the roast is small, cook for 3 hours.

Serve with your favorite sides.

Bake at 350 degrees. Serves 10, depending on the size of the pork roast you use.

Pork Stroganoff

Directions

Brown the meat, onion (cut up), Italian seasoning, fresh basil (cut up), oregano (cut up), and a sliced or cut-up mushrooms.

Add 1 can of mushroom soup, add 1 cup of milk. By this point the meat will have made a lot of juice to add to the mix. Add 3 tbs. of flour to a cup of water stir it up well. Now add to the steak mixture this will thicken the mixture. Now add the sour cream and stir in.

Cook up some noodles, drain, and serve pork stroganoff over the top of the noodles.

Serves 8.

Ingredients

5 pork steaks—cut up into chunks

1 tsp. basil—cut up

1 tsp. oregano—cut up

1 onion—diced up

1 tsp. Italian seasoning

1 16-oz. can of cream of mushroom soup

6-oz. can of mushrooms

3 tbs. of sour cream

Pulled Pork Sandwich

Ingredients

1 pork roast

4 onions—chopped up

4 tbs. butter

2 tsp. Italian seasoning

2 32-oz. containers of beef stock

2 tsp. of thyme

7 hamburger buns or hoagie rolls

2 tsp. basil—chopped

2 cloves of chopped-up garlic

Directions

Cook chopped up onions in butter and olive oil, Italian seasoning, 2 tsp. of fresh thyme. Cook mixture until the onions are brown. Now add the garlic and the two containers of beef stock and cook for another 20 minutes. Add this to the pork roast.

In a different pan, add the pork roast and brown on each side until you get nice brown on both sides. Take the baking pan or roaster and add the pork roast and let it cook for 5–6 hours. It should fall apart when taking it out of the pan.

Take the pork roast out of the pan and let rest so all the juices stay in the meat. When cool enough to touch take two forks and pull it apart.

Add back to the beef stock. Take some tongs and put on a hamburger bun or hoagie roll.

Serves 8.

Sausage Biscuits and Gravy

Ingredients

2 16-oz. pork sausage

1 onion—chopped

1 tsp. of basil—chopped

1 tsp. of thyme—chopped

1 lbs. package of bacon; cooked with the sausage—chopped

2 tbs. of butter

6 tbs. of flour

2 cups of milk

Directions

Make the biscuits up so they come out of the oven at the same time sausage gravy is done. You will find a recipe for biscuits in this cookbook.

In a frying pan, add 2: 16-oz. pork sausage, 1 chopped-up onion, 1 tsp. of chopped basil, 1 tsp. of thyme, 1 tsp. of oregano, 1 package of bacon—cooked with the sausage and chopped. Cook this mixture until the sausage and bacon are cooked. Now take out of the pan and drain, setting this aside until you get the gravy sauce done.

Take a couple tbs. of grease from the pan and drain the rest of the grease out of the pan.

Take the butter and bacon-sausage grease, adding it back into the pan. Add the flour to make the rue.

Add the two cups of milk to the rue using a whisk to stir. Add the sausage-bacon mixture back into the gravy. Just add over those homemade biscuits you just made.

Serves 8.

Scallop, Ham, and Potatoes

Directions

Fresh basil, 1 onion, and Italian seasoning. Cook until tender. Add to white sauce.

White sauce—butter, flour, salt, pepper to taste. Make up the rue. Add the butter, let it melt, then add the 6 tbs. of flour. Whisk them together, then add the milk. Cook until it starts to thicken. Add the cheese to mixture and stir until cheese is melted.

Get a 13 × 9 pan. Spray it with cooking spray. Add the sauce to the pan, then add a layer of potatoes and ham, then another layer of sauce and continue until all the sauce is in the pan. All the potatoes are layer in along with the ham. To top of the pan, you would add the rest of the cheese and bacon cover the whole top. Put it in the oven for 45 minutes until done. Bake at 350.

Serves 10.

Ingredients

5 cups ham chopped up

4 potatoes slice thinly

One cube butter

6 tbs. flour

2 cups of milk

2 cups mild cheddar

7 pieces of bacon—fried and chopped

1 tsp. of basil

1 tsp. of Italian seasoning

Sun-Dried Tomato and Pesto Vinaigrette Pork Chops

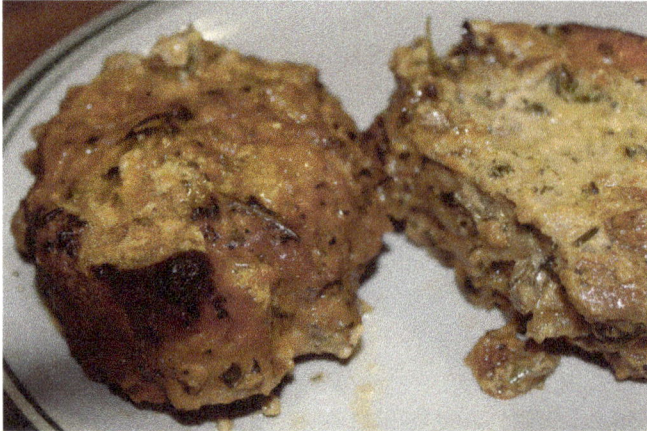

Ingredients

Brine for chops

8 2-inch pork chops

1 onion chopped up

2 tsp. fresh rosemary—chopped

2 tsp. thyme – fresh chopped up

2 tbs. basil stir in paste

1 tsp. of Italian seasoning

1 tsp. of garlic powder

2 tbs. olive oil

Directions

Mix all of this together in a small bowl. Take a large bowl and put some of the brine down on the bottom of the bowl. Layer in the pork chops, then brine. Repeat the process until the bowl is full cover and set in the fridge for about 1 hour.

Sauce

Ingredients

1 onion—chopped

1/4 cup of sun-dried tomato and pesto vinaigrette

1 tsp. of Italian seasoning

cube of butter

2 tbs. olive oil

1 tbs. of basil—stir in paste

2 tbs. of honey

1 tbs. molasses BBQ sauce

Directions

Mix all this together. Put this in frying pan and cook all this together until onions are soft and tender.

Add 3 cups of milk and stir with a whisk until all is mixed together. Cook over medium heat for a few minutes.

To thicken the sauce, add 2 tbs. flour to 1/2 of water into a small bowl mix well. Now add this to the sauce. If it seems a little thick, add 1/2 cup of water to mixture.

In a Dutch oven or baking dish, if you don't have one, put sauce on the bottom of the Dutch oven, then layer in the pork chops, sauce, and repeat the process until the pan is full. Leftover sauce pour over the top of the chops so it gets into every little small opening covering the chops completely.

Bake at 350 for 2 hours. Keep checking on it.

Serves 8–10.

Sweet and Sour Pork Steaks

Ingredients

8 pork steaks

2 tsp. of basil

1 tsp. of thyme

2 tsp. of oregano

1 onion—chopped

Directions

Cut up all the herbs and mix them up. Now take the pork steaks and put them into a bowl and put mixed up herbs on top. Layer pork steaks and herb mixture until all the pork steaks are gone. Now cover and put in the fridge until you get ready to cook them.

Sauce

Ingredients

3/4 cup of ketchup

1 tsp. of Worcestershire sauce

4 tbs. of vinegar

8 tbs. of sugar

2 tbs. of hoisin sauce

1 tbs. of molasses

1 chopped up onion

2 tbs. of brown sugar

Cook this about 4 minutes until smooth

Directions

Put the herb-covered pork steaks in the oven in a 13 × 9 baking dish.

Add the sauce on top and cook for about 35–40 minutes. Bake at 350.

Serves 8.

Roasted Ham

Directions

Zest the orange over the ham in the roaster. Then pour over the brown sugar and water mixed together. Add the hot butter rum and stir in the mixture. Now add the pineapple fresh if you can get it if not just use 1 can of chunk pineapple.

Add sliced orange over the top of the ham.

Bake on 350 degrees for 5 hours. Serve with your favorite sides.

Serves 10.

Ingredients

1 ham

1 zested orange

1 20-oz. can of pineapple—drained

1 cup brown sugar

3 cups of water

2 tbs. hot butter rum—(it comes in a container like whipped cream)

1 orange that you zested—sliced up

Teriyaki Pork Steak

Directions

Take the basil, the onion, and thyme. Mix together. Take the pork steaks and layer them with the mixture in a big bowl. When the bowl is filled up, put foil over the bowl. Let sit in in the fridge for 3 hours, or until you're ready to start cooking.

Sauce

Mix up half bottle of teriyaki sauce. Drain the pineapple, sweet honey barbecue sauce (1/2 cup), a 1/2 cup of brown sugar, and 1/2 cup of honey. Cook this until smooth for a few minutes.

Now take the bowl out of the fridge and take out the pork steaks and lay them out in a sprayed baking dish. Pour barbecue mixture over the pork steaks and cook for 3 hours at 350 degrees.

Ingredients

2 tsp. of basil—chopped

1 onion—chopped

1 tsp. of thyme—fresh chopped or use 1 tsp. of dried

8 pork steaks

1/2 a bottle Lawyers teriyaki sauce

1 can of pineapple chucks

1/2 cup of honey

1/2 cup brown sugar

1/2 cup honey BBQ sauce

Vegetables and Sides Dishes

Apple Sauce

Ingredients

1 bag of red apples—peeled and cut up into chunks

1 tsp. of cinnamon

1 tsp. of vanilla

1 cup of sugar

3 cups of water—to cover the apples

Directions

Add all the apples that you cut up into a big pot that you might cook stew in. Add in the sugar, cinnamon, and vanilla. Now add in the 3 cups of water and stir all the ingredients together.

Turn the stove on to med heat and let cook until all the apples are soft. Here's the fun part drain about two cups of juice out of the pan. Now take a mixer and mix everything until all the apples are smooth and there's no big chucks of apple in the apple sauce.

Your family will love this I serve this at Christmas time with whipped cream.

Serve 10 or more.

Alisha Bee Bee's Nutty Party Mix

Ingredients

1 box Corn Chex Square Cereal

1 box Rice Chex Square Cereal

1 large Can of Mixed Nuts

1 box of White Cheddar Mini Square Crackers

2 cups canola oil

4 tbs. Worchester sauce

1 tbs. garlic powder

1 tbs. Lawry's Seasoned alt

Directions

In a very large aluminum roaster pan, like you would use for your Thanksgiving turkey or large roasts, put all the dry ingredients in and mix it together well.

Take the oil, Worchester sauce, garlic powder, and seasoned salt, and mix that together in a 4-cup capacity measuring cup so you can mix well and pour over the dry ingredients in the large roasting pan.

Stir the cereal mix and oil/seasoning together carefully to keep all of it in the pan.

Preheat the oven to 250 degrees and place the pan with the Chex Mix in the oven and stir every 20 minutes for 2 hours. Each time you stir, make sure oil is getting to and through all the pieces of cereal. Take out of oven. Once you take it out, stir it occasionally until cool enough to store in a large container.

Serves a crowd.

Mashed Potatoes

Directions

Boil the potatoes in butter water until tender. Next, drain and put into a bowl add basil, mayo, butter, salt, and milk and mix with a mixer.

Serves 10.

Ingredients

15 potatoes

1 tsp. of basil—dried

2 tbs. of mayo

3 tbs. of butter

1/2 tsp. of salt

1/2 cup of milk

Potato Salad

Ingredients

7 potatoes—put in a pot to boil about 20 minutes

10 eggs—boiled, peeled, and chopped

1 onion—diced

1 cup of mayo

2 tbs. of mustard

4 stalks of celery—finely chopped

2 tbs. of pickle juice

1 16-oz. can of black olives—drained

1 tsp. fresh basil

A pinch of oregano—1/2 tsp

1/2 cup of ranch dressing

Directions

Peel the potatoes and chop up into chunks. Add to a bowl, chop up the onion and add 4 stalks of celery (finely chopped) to the bowl. Peel and cut up the eggs add them to the bowl. Now add the black olives to the bowl.

Sauce

I cup a mayo, 2 tbs. of mustard, 2 tbs. of pickle juice, 1 tsp. basil (fresh), a pinch of oregano (1/2 tsp.) 1/2 cup of ranch dressing. Mix together and pour over the potato salad. I mix this up with a big spoon until all is mixed in. Add salt and pepper to taste.

Serves 10.

Rosemary and Onions Potatoes

Directions

Take and cut up the potatoes in slices and set aside. Chop the onion and set aside. Chop the fresh basil and rosemary and set that aside.

Take cookie sheet and add the potatoes and onions, basil, Italian seasoning, and sprinkle with olive oil and add salt and pepper to taste. Mix it all together and let set for about 10 minutes.

Bake at 350 for about 20 minutes. Stir the mixture a couple of time during baking.

Serves 8.

Ingredients

1/2 bag of small 2 lbs., red potatoes—cut in half

1 onion—chopped

2 tbs. of rosemary—cut up fine

2 tbs. of olive oil

2 tbs. basil—chopped

1 tsp. of Italian seasoning

Salt and pepper to taste

Salads and Pastas

Apple Chicken Salad

Directions

Mix all the ingredients from above, then add the sauce or use the salad dressing you love.

Serves 6.

Ingredients

1/2 bag of salad mix—you choose which kind you like

1 apple—chopped

2 tsp. of basil—chopped

1 cup grapes—cut in half

1/2 cup dried cranberry and walnuts

2 cups cooked chicken—chopped

1 tomato—sliced

Sauce

1/2 cup ranch

3 tbs. of honey—mix or use your favorite salad dressing (Optional)

Broccoli Salad

Ingredients

1 tsp. of Italian seasoning

1/2 cup of hoisin with garlic

1/2 cup teriyaki

1 onion—chopped

3 cups of broccoli—chopped

1 cup of carrots—chopped

2 tsp. of basil—chopped

2 packs of maple-flavored bacon—chopped and fried

1 tsp. of sesame seed oil

1 tsp. of olive oil

1 tsp. of thyme—chopped

1 tsp. of fresh rosemary—chopped

1 tsp. of oregano

Directions

Sauce

Take the of Italian seasoning, hoisin with garlic, teriyaki, onion, basil, sesame seed oil, olive oil, thyme, rosemary, oregano. Mix this all together and cook for 5 minutes on the stove so all the flavors marry together. Put in the fridge and let cool to almost cold.

Cut up all the broccoli, carrots, and onion. Cut up all the bacon into chunks and put into a big bowl. Now add the sauce that has been sitting in the fridge. Pour over the top. Mix it well.

Serves 15.

Chicken Asian Noodle Salad

1 tsp. fresh oregano (chopped), 1 tsp. fresh thyme (chopped), 1 tsp. Italian seasoning, 1 tsp. poultry seasoning. Cook this all together until the chicken is done. Take chicken out of stock and put in fridge to cool. When the stock is cooled off, put the stock into a container and put into the freezer to be used a later date.

Next, cook the noodles, broccoli, and carrots together, adding a bit of oil to keep the noodles from sticking together. When done, which only takes a couple of minutes, drain the noodles, broccoli, and carrots. Set aside.

Ingredients

1 small package of spaghetti noodles—cooked

2 cups of broccoli—cooked

1 cup of carrots

8 pieces of chicken

2 cloves of garlic—grated

1/4 cup of brown sugar

1/4 cup soy sauce

2 tbs. hoisin sauce

2 tbs. sesame oil

1/4 tsp. of ginger

2 onions—chopped

1 tsp. of fresh basil—chopped

1 tsp. oregano

1 32-oz. container of chicken stock

1 tsp. fresh thyme—chopped

1 tsp. Italian seasoning

1 tsp. poultry seasoning

Directions

Cook the chicken in the chicken stock, 1 onion (chopped), 1 tsp. of fresh basil (chopped).

Sauce

Ingredients

1/4 cup of brown sugar

1/4 cup soy sauce

2 tbs. hoisin sauce

2 tbs. sesame oil

1/4 tsp. of ginger

1 tbs. of mandarin sauce

1 onion—chopped

Directions

Now cook all the sauce ingredients for a few minutes to marry all the flavors together.

Now that the chicken is cool enough to touch, cut up the chicken into chunks and put into a very large bowl. The chicken was already cooked in all the herbs so it's full of flavor.

Add the noodle mixture and mix up with a spoon.

Pour over the sauce and mix up with all the other ingredients.

Serves 9.

Chicken Tomato Pasta Salad

Ingredients

7 pieces of chicken—cooked in butter and olive oil

1 tsp. of fresh thyme—chopped

1 container of cherry tomatoes—cut in half; yellow and red

3 tsp. of basil—chopped

2 onions—chopped

3 cups—cooked egg noodles

2 tsp. of oregano

1 tsp. of dried Italian seasoning

1 lbs. package of maple-flavored bacon—cooked and chopped

1 1/2 cups broccoli—cut into smaller pieces

1 cup of carrots—cut into smaller pieces so they are bite size

Directions

Take the chicken that's all cut up and put with onion, basil, oregano, thyme, and poultry seasoning. Mix with olive oil and set in fridge for about 1 hour.

Now cook the noodles for about 7 minutes. When done, set them aside after they are drained.

Take the chicken out of the fridge and cook in 3 tbs. of butter and 3 tbs. of olive oil. Remember, the chicken has all those herbs in it already. Now add the mushrooms and let the chicken finish cooking with the mushrooms for about 10–15 minutes total time take out and drain and set aside.

Sauce

Take the tomato and slice them in half and add, 1 tsp. of thyme-fresh chopped up, 3 tsp. of basil-cut up, 1 onion (chopped), 2 tsp. of oregano (cut up), 1 tsp. of dried Italian seasoning, and 2 tsp. of olive oil. Add the broccoli and carrots to this mix this up together and set aside. Precook the broccoli and carrots about 6 minutes and drain.

In a big bowl, add the chicken mixture to the noodles. Add the tomato mixture and mix all together top with a little basil to give it a finished look. Top with the bacon (fried, cut up).

Serves 10.

Crab and Shrimp Salad

Ingredients

2 lbs. of shrimp

6 eggs—boiled; chopped

1 package imitation crab—cut into chucks

1 can of olives—cut in half

1 onion—chopped

3 stalks of celery—cut into very small pieces

1 half head of lettuce—chopped

2 tomatoes—chopped

1 tsp. of Italian seasoning

1 tsp. of basil—chopped

Directions

In a very large bowl, add the lettuce that is chopped up and 6 eggs (boiled; chopped). Next add the shrimp and crab.

Add the olives cut into half, chopped up 1 peeled onion, 3 stalks of celery cut up fine, 2 tomatoes chopped up.

Sauce

1 1/2 cups of mayo—best foods, 1/2 cup of ranch dressing, add the Italian seasoning, 1 tsp. of basil mix all together.

Time to put this all together take the salad you just made add the sauce to the salad with a big spoon and mix well. Chill in the fridge until you're ready to serve dinner. Remember, the longer this sits in the fridge, the better it will taste, as the flavors will all marry together.

Fruit Salad

Directions

Take everything from above and cut it up putting it into a large mixing bowl. You will need a large bowl for this. Mix everything together and put into the fridge until you're ready to serve it.

Serves 15.

Ingredients

1 orange—peeled and cut up

3 cups of watermelon—cut up

1 cup of strawberries—cut up

1 cup of blueberries

5 apples cut up

1 small pineapple—peeled and cut up

4 bananas—cut up

1 tsp. of vanilla

1/2 tsp. of cinnamon

1/2 cup of sugar

Grilled Chicken Salad

Directions

Put the chicken in the oven with salt and pepper and cook in the oven until chicken is done and brown on both sides. Cook at 350 degrees for about 30 minutes or until done. Cut up into cubes and set aside.

Take the garlic bread. Bake in the oven until brown. Cut it up into cubes and set aside (garlic croutons work too).

Remember, all ingredients need to be chopped up, including the bacon. I usually just panfry the bacon, cut it up, and add it to the salad.

Mix all the salad veggies together in a large bowl, then add chicken to the salad along with garlic bread, adding your favorite salad dressing on top.

Serves 10.

Ingredients

1 loaf of garlic bread

2 containers of cherry red and yellow tomatoes—cut in half

6 grilled thighs

1 lbs. pack of maple-favored bacon

3 large carrots—shredded

3 large stalks of celery—chopped

2 tsp. of Basil—chopped

2 large avocados

1 can of black olives—cut in half (optional)

1 small package salad mix

1 onion—finely chopped

1 tsp. Italian seasoning

15 mushrooms—sliced up

1 8-oz. pack of cheese—grated

Salad Dressing (Optional)

Package ranch and 3 tbs. of honey, mixed up

Ham Salad

Directions

Put salad mix in a big bowl. Add yellow and red cherry tomatoes cut in half.

Now add the avocados cut up and place in the salad bowl.

Add the basil (chopped), olives, chopped-up ham, and one onion (chopped).

Sprinkle of cheese.

Sauce

Half cup of ranch and 4 tbs. of honey mix well as the honey is thick.

Ingredients

1 bag of salad mix

1 container of yellow and red cherry tomatoes—cut in half

2 avocados chopped up (optional)

1 tsp. of basil—chopped

1 cup chopped-up ham

1 16-oz. can whole black of olives

1 onion—chopped

Sprinkle with a bit of grated cheese

Ramen Chicken Salad

Ingredients

10 pieces of chicken

1 onion that I chopped up

2 tsp. of fresh basil – chopped up fine

1 tsp. Italian seasoning

2 tbs. olive oil

1 tsp. poultry seasoning

2 cups flour—with Italian seasoning, 1 tsp. dried basil

Directions

Take all the chicken, onion that is chopped up, fresh basil, Italian seasoning, olive oil, poultry seasoning mix all together with chicken. Set aside in the fridge for 1 hour.

Take the 2 cups of flour. Add with Italian seasoning and 1 tsp. dried basil. Mix all together to panfry the chicken. Brown on both sides until golden brown. put into the oven and bake at 350 for 25 minutes. The chicken should almost be done when you put this into the oven. This allows you to get the rest of your dinner done.

With the leftover chicken, let's make a salad.

Cook ramen noodles in the microwave until done. Drain the noodles.

Cut up the chicken into chunks and sprinkle some basil over the noodles. Sprinkle Italian seasoning over the top. Cut up an avocado and add to the mix. Cut up the tomato into chunks. Mix all together with the ramen noodles.

Sauce

In a tiny bowl, add 2 tbs. of hoisin sauce and 1 tsp. of sesame oil. Mix together.

Sprinkle over the top of salad and sit and enjoy.

Teriyaki Chicken Noodles

Directions

Cut up the chicken brown in olive oil and butter until done, then take them out of the pan and set it aside.

Cook up the noodles in butter so they don't stick together. When they are done, take them and set them aside.

Sauce

In a bowl, add oregano, basil, sesame seed, mandarin teriyaki sauce, hoisin sauce, dried garlic, honey, and soy sauce. Mix all this together until smooth.

Now add the chicken to the drained noodles along with the sauce, peas, and carrots. Let it cook on medium heat until it bubbles, then turn down to low for about 35 minutes. Serve with garlic bread.

Serves 8.

Ingredients

1 package spaghetti noodles

4 chicken breasts—cooked and cut up

1 small package of peas and carrots

1 tsp. of oregano

1 tsp. of basil

1 onion—diced

1 tsp. of pure sesame seed oil

3 tbs. mandarin teriyaki sauce

2 tsp. of hoisin sauce

1 tsp. of garlic—dried

1/4 cup honey

1 tsp. soy sauce

1 tsp. poultry season

Tortellini Salad

Directions

Cook the tortellini per instructions and cool in cold water and drain. In a big bowl, add the tortellini, olives cut in half, cumbers sliced up, red onion sliced in slices and separated. Now add the one container of small red tomatoes, 2 tbs. of fresh basil chopped up, now add the 1 tsp. of Italian seasoning, one clove of garlic chopped up. Add salad dressing just before you serve.

Ingredients

1 package tortellini sausage—boiled for 10–15 minutes

1 can of olives—cut in half

2 cumbers—slice up

1 red onion—sliced up

1 container red tomatoes—small

2 tbs. fresh basil—chopped

1 tsp. Italian seasoning

1 clove of garlic—chopped

Salad dressing (Optional)—drizzle over the salad just before you serve. (I used Honey and ranched mixed together as this is my families favorite dressing

Soups

Chicken Soup

Directions

Add the chicken to the chicken stock, mixed veggies, 1 onion, and 1 can of cream chicken soup.

1 tsp. poultry seasoning, salt and pepper to taste, and a package of chicken gravy. Mix all together. Cook on the stove for 35 minutes on medium heat.

Now add the noodles to the chicken mixture and serve.

Ingredients

3 cups of chicken—cut up

2 32-oz. containers of chicken stock

2 12-oz. packages a blend of broccoli, carrots, and cauliflower

1 onion—cut up

1 16-oz. can of cream of chicken soup

1 tsp. of poultry seasoning

Salt and pepper to taste

One package of chicken gravy

1 tsp. of basil

2 cups of noodles—boiled with 1 tsp. of butter

French Onion Soup

Directions

Cook onions in butter and olive oil. Add basil, oregano, and thyme together until onions are brown and tender. Add 2 containers of beef stock and beef paste. Let cook for about 2 hours. Cook on medium heat until done.

You can put this in a bowl and top with cheese and toast. I cook with french onion soup for a beef roast or a pork roast.

Serves 8.

Ingredients

4 onions—diced up

1/2 stick of butter

2 containers of beef stock 32 oz.

1 tsp. basil chopped finely

2 tsp. of thyme

2 cloves of garlic

2 tsp. of beef paste

Turkey

Roasted Turkey and Dressing

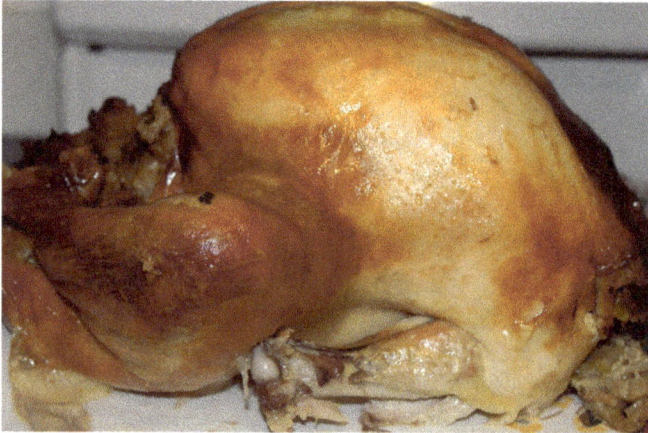

Ingredients

25 lbs. turkey (adjust size of turkey for your family)

2 apples—peeled and diced up

4 stalks of celery—diced

1 onion—peeled and cut up

4 packs bread stuffing

2 cups ham—chopped

4 eggs

2 32-oz. cans of chicken stock

1 package turkey gravy

1 tsp. of sage

1 tsp. of chopped up sage

1 tsp. of thyme—chopped

1 tsp. rosemary—chopped

Salt and pepper to taste

2 tbs. of butter

Directions

Take the giblets from the turkey and boil them in butter and 2 containers of chicken stock. Until they are done. Set them aside.

Cook up onions, celery, sage, thyme, rosemary in butter, and olive oil until they are almost soft, then set this aside.

Get the bread and stuffing. Add all the herbs, onion mixture, then apples.

Now take the giblets and cut them up and add this to the dressing. Mix all this together with your hands or a big spoon.

Add in the rest of the stock from the pan to the dressing next add in turkey gravy package stir this all together. Next add in the ham. Mix together.

Directions for Turkey

Take the turkey and raise out the turkey place into a roaster or deep baking dish. Stuff the turkey with the dressing.

(Author's note: If you don't stuff your turkey, then put stuffing in a 13 × 9 baking dish. Put foil over the top. Put this into the fridge until 1 hour before the turkey is done, then put into the oven at 350 for 45 minutes.)

Put foil over the wings so they don't burn. Pat dry the turkey add soften butter all over the turkey. Add in remaining chicken stock in the roaster put the lid on the roaster let cook for 6 hours. Keep basting the turkey with melted butter every hour.

Making sure the turkey doesn't lose any chicken stock if it does just add more if you need to.

Roast at 350 for 6 hours.

Turkey Gravy

Ingredients

3 cups of turkey—cut up

1 can cream chicken soup

1 onion—cut up

2 tsp. of poultry seasoning

1 tsp. of thyme—dried

1 tsp. of basil—cut up

1 tsp. of sage

2 stalks of celery—cut up

4 carrots—sliced up

2 containers of either chicken stock or turkey stock

Mashed Potatoes

8 potatoes—boiled sliced in half to cook easy

1 tbs. of mayo

2 tbs. of butter

1/2 cup of milk (I use lactose-free milk when I use milk)

Salt and pepper to taste

Directions

There are many things to do with leftover turkey when you make it like soup, casseroles, turkey and dumplings, or turkey gravy.

This time its turkey gravy served over mashed potatoes which my family loves.

Now add all the ingredients together under directions and let boil for 30 minutes to make sure all the herbs marry together.

To make the gravy, add a 1/2 cup of flour and about 1 cup of water together mix well. This way there are no lumps in the flour mixture. Pour the flour mix into the turkey stock with all the turkey and veggies.

Keep stirring—this will thicken fast. If it thickens too, much add some water to thin it down to what you want.

Directions

Drain the potatoes, then add all the ingredients for mashed potatoes beat with a mixer well until all the potatoes are mixed in.

Get a big scoop of the turkey gravy and pour over the top. Add salt and pepper to taste.

Serves 10.

Index

www.ingramcontent.com/pod-product-compliance
Lightning Source LLC
Chambersburg PA
CBHW040317100426
42811CB00012B/1470